Gilbert
VanZandt
The story of a Civil War drummer boy and his pony, Fannie Lee

Gilbert VanZandt

The story of a Civil War
drummer boy
and his pony, Fannie Lee

Marilyn W. Seguin

Brandenbooks
Boston

© Copyright 2006
By Marilyn W. Seguin

Library of Congress Cataloging-in-Publication Data

Seguin, Marilyn.
   Gilbert VanZandt : the story of Civil War drummer boy and his pony, Fannie Lee / Marilyn W. Seguin.
      p. cm.
   Includes bibliographical references.
   ISBN 0-8283-2116-7 (alk. paper)
   1. VanZandt, Gilbert, 1851-1944--Juvenile literature.
   2. Child soldiers--Ohio--Biography--Juvenile literature.
   3. Drummers (Musicians)—Ohio--Biography--Juvenile literature.
   4. Ponies--Ohio--Juvenile literature.
   5. United States. Army. Ohio Infantry Regiment, 79th (1862-1865)--Juvenile literature.
   6. United States--History--Civil War, 1861-1865--Participation, Juvenile--Juvenile literature.
   7. United States--History--Civil War, 1861-1865--Campaigns--Juvenile literature. I. Title.

E525.579th .S44 2006
973.7'471092--dc22
[B]
                                    2006013521

BRANDEN BOOKS
Division of Branden Publishing Company
**PO Box 812094
Wellesley, MA 02482**

This book is dedicated to
Kevin Markee (1955-2005)

Contents

List of illustrations 11
Timeline of events in the military service of
   Gilbert VanZandt 13
Introduction by Gary Kersey 15
Chapter One: War Drums 19
Chapter Two: Drumming All the Way 25
Chapter Three: Camp Dennison 31
Chapter Four: Billy and Banjo 41
Chapter Five: "It hain't hurt me yet" 49
Chapter Six: Battle of Resaca 53
Chapter Seven: Fighting at Kennesaw Mountain 59
Chapter Eight: Sherman's Bummers 65
Chapter Nine: Battle of Peach Tree Creek 73
Chapter Ten: The Fall of Atlanta 81
Chapter Eleven: Incident at Ebenezer Creek 87
Chapter Twelve: "He knew no fear" 93
Chapter Thirteen: On to Washington 97
Chapter Fourteen: An Interview with the President 101
Author's Note and Acknowledgments 111
"Little Gib" poem by W. C. Ticheno 115
Civil War Glossary 123
Sources 125
More information 127

List of Illustrations

Map of Civil War 17
Property map of Port William 29
Troops crossing the Ohio River 38
Drummer boys beating out tattoo in camp...........................39
Document showing Lil' Gib's age at enlistment...................40
Drummer boys playing cards in camp 52
Shelling of the railroad near Resaca 58
"The Rogue's March" 64
General William Tecumseh Sherman....................................70
Map showing drive to Atlanta 71
General Sherman in council during siege of Atlanta 79
Sherman's men tearing up railroad tracks in Atlanta............83
Freed slaves welcoming Union army....................................86
Map showing march from Atlanta to Savannah....................92
Libby Prison...100
The Grand Review 104, 105
Gib's enlistment record...106
President Andrew Johnson..110
Historical marker recognizing Lil Gib 121

Timeline of events in the military service of Gilbert VanZandt, born on December 20, 1851, in Port William, Ohio, to John and Nancy VanZandt

1861   Beginning of American Civil War, "The War Between the States," April 14.

1862   Gilbert signs on to "drum up" recruits for the Union army, July. Enlists with Company D, 79th Ohio Volunteer Regiment as its drummer, August 6. "Lil Gib" officially mustered in on Oct. 31; ordered to Kentucky Sept. 3.

1863   Duty in Tennessee until Feb. 1864.

1864   Atlanta Campaign May 2-Sept. 8; Battle of Resaca May 14-15; Assault on Kennesaw Mt. June 27; Peach Tree Creek July 19-20; Occupation of Atlanta Sept. 2-Nov. 15; March to the Sea Nov. 15-Dec. 10; Siege of Savannah Dec. 10-21.

1865   Campaign of the Carolinas Jan. to April; General Lee surrenders to General Grant at Appomattox Court House April 9; President Lincoln is assassinated April 14; March to Washington D.C. via Richmond, Va. April 29-May 20; Grand Review May 24; Mustered out June 9.

Introduction

What would life be like for a 10-year-old drummer boy serving in the American Civil War? Well, essentially the same as for any enlistee in the army! There was little opportunity to shield anyone from either the good or bad experiences of war. There were playmaking, pranks, jokes, marches, and battles - as well as carrying the wounded and burying the dead.

Courage is something we commonly ascribe to adults - not children. But in this instance, Gilbert VanZandt, known as Lil Gib, must be recognized for unusual valor and patriotism - uncommon at any time, in any war.

Marilyn Seguin carefully layers the experiences of Lil Gib, the drummer boy of the 79th Ohio OVI. The true history of the outfit is carefully interwoven with the anecdotal. It is a delicate balance - but the author does great work and makes the story of Lil Gib a memorable read.

The real life Civil War story of Gilbert VanZandt is one that needed to be told.

This new book, *Gilbert VanZandt,* offers another remembrance to all the very young who served in the American Civil War.

Gary Kersey
Civil War Historian and Storyteller
Wilmington, Ohio

Hark! I hear the tramp of thousands,
And of armed men the hum;
Lo! A nation's hosts have gathered
Round the quick alarming drum,--
Saying, "Come, Freemen, come!
Ere your heritage be wasted," said the quick
Alarming drum.

Bret Harte, *Reveille*

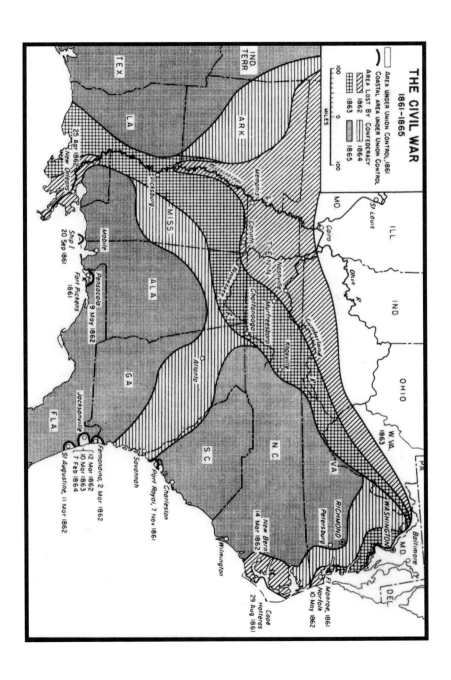

Chapter One

War Drums

Gib tapped out a rhythm with a pencil on top of his school desk in time with the spring rain beating against the window glass Rata tat tat went the pencil in syncopation with the rain. Gib had always been able to feel a rhythm of his own, and he could hear things that others did not. Gib had been hammering away on things since he could walk. Finally, his parents had given him a small snare drum for his birthday. Still tapping, he turned his attention to his teacher, Mr. Bodkin, who was in the middle of a geography lesson.

"The most intense fighting took place along a little country lane known as "the hornet's nest," said Mr. Bodkin. A great battle had been fought last month at Shiloh, in Tennessee. "Johnston's Secesh forces attacked our troops, led by General Grant, for almost two days. But the Union prevailed!"

Gib listened intently as Mr. Bodkin talked on about far away places with strange names—Ball's Bluff and Bull Run and Fort Sumter. This war business all seemed a great adventure to Gib and he wished that he could be a solider, but everyone said that the war would soon be over. At any rate, a boy had to be 18 to enlist and Gib, born Gilbert VanZandt, was only ten. Gib thought that if he couldn't be a solider, maybe he would be a teacher like Mr. Bodkin so he could at least study soldiery. His father wanted to teach Gib how to make shoes, but Gib didn't want to learn that dull business. He wanted to go places and do great things. He wanted to be a soldier!

Why even when he slept, Gib dreamed of adventure. In his dreams he went to all of the places he could not go when he was awake. Sometimes upon awakening, Gib would write his dreams so that he could extend his adventure into his waking hours. In this way Gib had gone swimming in a pool as green as the new corn that grew in the fields of Port William. He had wandered through mansions filled with tables piled high with strange, rich foods. He had met kings and queens and frolicked with animals that he had never seen in his waking. Once he had ridden a blue pony across a desert plain, being chased by murderous thieves, but he had not been caught. Somehow his dreams made bearable his waking life of sameness. For only in his sleep could he experience excitement and adventure.

In the seat next to him, Anna, his 8-year-old sister, cleared her throat to get his attention.

"Shush," she mouthed at him, frowning at his tapping pencil. Gib winked at Anna and kept on tapping just to annoy her. Suddenly something sharp poked into his back, making him sit up straight.

"Stop that tapping, Lil Gib, or I'll make you wish you had!" a voice hissed in his ear.

It was Masie Furnace. Masie called him "Lil Gib" on account of his size. Although he was two years older than Masie, she was nearly six inches taller. She'd hated him ever since he had saved her from drowning in the stone bottomed swimming hole they called the Old Goggle. Embarrassed her, it had, because he'd found out she couldn't swim. When he teased her about it, she retaliated by making fun of his size.

"You think you're such a big man for saving me, don't you Gib? Well, you're not big—you're little. Little Gib. Lil Gib. That's what I'll call you from now on!" Masie had said after she'd choked up water and caught her breath.

What did it matter if he was small for his age, Gib thought? He had been brave enough to jump into Old Goggle and drag her out screaming and flailing, hadn't he? But the nickname had caught on, and now even Anna called him Lil Gib sometimes. He pretended not to care, but it was hurtful. Their father, a shoemaker, had made Gib a pair of shoes with thick heels and soles that made him a little taller, but Gib was still the smallest 10-year-old boy in the school. Gib sighed and stopped his pencil tapping.

Mr. Bodkin asked for a volunteer to locate the state of Tennessee on the map mounted on the wall. Masie raised her hand.

"I can find Tennessee," she declared, "because that's where my brother's last letter came from." Masie was such a know-it-all, Gib thought, as he watched her trot to the front of the room and, with a smug look on her face she pointed out the state of Tennessee.

"Right here--this is where my brother is soldiering for the cause!" said Masie. She sure was full of herself, Gib thought.

Masie's brother, 18-year-old John Furnace, had been one of the first volunteers from the little town of Port William, Ohio. Everyone in Port William was mighty proud of John Furnace, and its citizens had given him a grand send off when he enlisted. Gib was proud of him too, even if John was nasty Masie's brother.

Masie made a face at Gib as she passed him on the way back to her seat.

"If my father goes to war, I am going with him," he said to Masie under his breath. He'd show Masie Furnace a thing or two when he followed his anger at the Seceshes into the Army of the United States. That is, if the war lasted long enough. Why the nerve of those southern states, thinking they could break up the United States!

"I don't care if you do, Lil Gib," said Masie angrily.

After Mr. Bodkin finished the geography lesson, he dismissed the class. Gib and Anna left the neat brick building and walked together down Walnut Street, past the pretty Baptist church and down the alley toward the house on Main Street in which they'd lived all their lives.

That evening over supper with their parents, the talk was again about war.

"News is that the War Department will open its recruiting offices again next month," said John VanZandt, as he passed the platter of roasted chicken to his wife Nancy. Gib and Anna listened carefully—war news was important to everyone in Port William—young and old. Nearby, baby brother Will began to cry in his cradle.

"Still, everyone is saying the war can't last much longer," Nancy replied, getting up from the table to tend the baby. Everyone expected the war to be a short one because last month the War Department had closed its recruiting offices. It seemed that no more soldiers would be needed. Perhaps the early volunteers would be enough, they'd thought. But now it was May of 1862, and the news was that more recruiting would be needed after all.

"I'm of a mind to enlist just so's to speed things up," said John VanZandt. Nancy gave him an anxious look but did not say anything.

Over the past year Gib had watched some of the boys of Port William, mostly the 18- and 19-year-olds, march off as the recruiters came to town. But Gib's father, who was then 32, had not enlisted with them because Nancy had convinced him he could serve the war effort in other ways.

"You are the best shoemaker in Clinton County, and our soldiers need good, sturdy shoes for the long marches. It's as good to serve the cause as a shoemaker as a soldier," she said. John had not enlisted in those early days of the war, and he continued to work in the tiny shop behind their house making shoes. Gib sometimes helped his father stretch the soft leather into shape for the tops. Then holes were punched and the leather was sewn with steel needles threaded with strong linen or flax fibers. Finally, the thick, sturdy soles were pegged or stitched to the tops.

But today it seemed that more men were needed to finish putting down the Rebellion, and Gib knew his father really wanted to leave shoemaking behind and go to war.

"My brothers and I have talked this over, and we are of the same mind, Nancy," said Gib's father. John had four brothers. Two of them had enlisted earlier in the war. "We plan to enlist together. And my brother Tom will take both his boys with him."

Gib's mother was silent. No one wanted to see loved ones go off to war, perhaps never to return. Yet feelings of patriotism ran strong in Nancy and "Save the Union" was the rallying cry for everyone in Port William. Gib's mother had cheered as her own two young brothers marched out of town when the recruiters last came. And then she had gone home and wept.

"And what of the business, John, how will I manage it if you march off to war?" Most of the citizens of little Port William were merchants or farmers. If the men were to enlist and leave their stores and farms, only the women, children, and a few old men would be left to carry on with farming and business.

Gib wondered if his mother knew how to make shoes. Gib had watched his father working at the shop at the back of their Main Street house often enough, as John crafted boots with slight heels, and shoes with spool heels, and soft, kidskin house slippers to be worn inside. His father had been one of the first shoemakers in the county to craft a pair of shoes that distinguished between the shapes of the right foot and the left foot. Until then, everyone had worn two of the same shape shoes.

"Some sacrifices will have to be made. The blood of soldiers runs in our veins, yours and mine, Nancy. Our ancestors fought in the Revolutionary War and the War of 1812 to preserve our freedom. I feel now it is my turn to do my part," he said.

"Then go if you must," said Nancy, and she left the room, taking the now silent baby with her.

"I aim to," said John.

Gilbert VanZandt, ten years old, knew that the blood of a soldier also ran in his veins. And it wasn't enough for Gib to be the son or grandson or nephew or cousin of a soldier. He would BE a soldier.

"And I am going with you!" Gib shouted.

Chapter Two

Drumming All the Way

In July of 1862, the citizens of Port William got word that a recruiting detail was coming to town. Notices were posted that a war meeting would be held in the schoolhouse. Dozens of signs were nailed to storefronts and trees announcing the meeting:

Down with the Rebellion
Volunteers Wanted
Able Bodied Men for the 79th Ohio Volunteer Infantry
Where they will enlist all who would like to rally around the
OLD STARS AND STRIPES,
the emblem of America's Freedom
$100 Bounty! Regular Army pay and Rations
to commence on taking the oath.
The Subscribers having been appointed Recruiting Officers,
will open a Recruiting Office at the Port William Schoolhouse

   The Port William women, including Nancy VanZandt, got together to plan a lavish hog roast as a send-off to those who decided to enlist.
   "Gib, Anna: take this pail and fill it with blackberries from those bushes by the edge of the millstream. I'm aiming to make a cobbler for the feast," said Nancy, on the day of the meeting. Gib and Anna scampered off to do as their mother asked, and they had a pail full of blackberries in no time. Other families would contribute what they could—jars of pickles, the first ripe

tomatoes from the garden, fresh eggs, and hot bread with apple butter preserved from last fall's fruit. For most, the contribution would mean less food to eat during the winter months to come, when supplies might be scarce. Many of the farmers who planned to enlist today would leave the women and young children to harvest and preserve what had been planted the previous spring. The merchants had stockpiled their wares for the women to sell while they were gone. But no one expected the war to last much longer. The hope was that the men would return before spring planting.

That afternoon, Gib climbed high into a tree to watch for the recruiting detail. He wanted to be the first person in Port William to see the parade! He wasn't there long before he spotted the detail crossing Andersons Fork Stream--four soldiers on horseback, and a fifth soldier driving a six-mule team, pulling a wagon full of patriotic bunting. Quickly, Gib climbed down the tree and ran to the house for his drum.

As the officer and his enlisted men rode into town, Gib stood beside the road and enthusiastically beat out a rhythm on the snare. Soon someone began to play on a fife, and the band of two fell into line ahead of the recruiting detail as they marched proudly through the town. The soldiers looked grand in their dark blue uniforms with shiny brass buttons, and they sat tall in their saddles. They proceeded down Main Street to Third Street, and as they passed each house, the citizens streamed out of their homes, cheering, and followed them to the schoolhouse. Children danced and dogs barked. Gib drummed all the way.

By the time the recruiting detail reached Walnut Street, nearly every citizen and dog of Port William had joined the parade. At the schoolhouse, the soldiers dismounted and went inside. Port William was alive with excitement as everyone filled the building to overflowing. Gib recognized all of his neighbors: he saw the Preacher Leittler and his family, and his neighbors, the Weeks and Orleys and Gallaghers. He saw his aunts and uncles and his cousins. Even the dreadful Masie Furnace was there with her parents and baby brother. Why, everyone he knew in this world was there at the meeting he realized.

The crowd fell silent as the officer, Lieutenant Ellwood, began to speak. Lieutenant Ellwood wore a perfectly cut dark blue uniform with big, gold buttons. His pants were lighter blue, and his shiny black boots gleamed from recent polishing. He wore tan gloves and a dark blue kepi with a black leather bill. Gib thought Lieutenant Ellwood looked grand!

"Men of Port William, your country calls you to its service! You are needed to help put down the late Rebellion! It is better to fall in this cause than live to see our proud country rent asunder and dismantled of its glory! Home is sweet and freedom is dear! The strength of our nation is to be tried with this War. Come all you men who are able! Fight for the Union!"

And as the citizens cheered, Lieutenant Ellwood smiled at Gib and flipped him a coin.

"That's for drumming today," said Lieutenant Ellwood.

Gib fingered the coin—it was a 50 cent piece and he had earned it with his drum! Gib pocketed the coin. Tonight he would remove the top of his drum and stash the coin inside for safekeeping.

When Lieutenant Ellwood finished his speech, the fifer played "The Battle Hymn of the Republic," and Gib, beating once again on his drum, thought he would burst with pride.

Then Lieutenant Ellwood began to move around the schoolroom, calling for volunteers to step into the line behind him. Gib began to beat on his drum once again.

"Step up, men of Port William. Step up and join the cause!" shouted Lieutenant Ellwood. One by one, Gib watched as the men and boys of Port William joined the line and marched in a circle around the room as he continued to beat upon his little drum.

Gib's father was one of the first to join the march and Gib marched beside him. Then Mr. Bodkin stepped in line. When the march was done, 20 young men of the neighborhood—farmers, clerks, merchants—had volunteered to enlist. The group included five VanZandts, and Gib intended to make it six!

"Father, I am going with you," said Gib when the time came to sign the enlistment forms.

"You'll do no such thing, Gib. You're much too young for soldiering," said his father.

"I'll enlist as a drummer, not a soldier," said Gib. If the tide would not carry him forward, then he would just have to paddle his own boat, thought Gib.

"Your mother'll be needing you here now, son. I'm counting on you," said his father.

"Maybe there is a way you can do your part for the cause," said Lieutenant Ellwood. "Perhaps your mother would let you drum for the new recruits at Fort Dennison. Then, once their training's over, we'll send you back to your Ma."

"We'll ask your Ma," said John VanZandt. After everyone had finished stuffing themselves with the roast pork, preserves, salads, cobbler and pies, Gib told his mother of Lieutenant Ellwood's invitation to drum for the recruits.

"You'll do no such thing, Gilbert VanZandt," said his mother. Wasn't it enough that she had given two brothers and a husband to the war effort? Gib cast his father a pleading look.

"It's just for the recruiting and training, Nancy. When we march off to do the fighting, I'll send Gib back to you. It won't be for long. The little fellow will surely tire of camp life," said John.

So in the end, Nancy consented to let her boy go off with the men of Port William, fully expecting to see him back home in a few weeks. As Gib marched proudly through the streets of Port William that evening, he saw Masie Furnace watching him. Without missing a beat, he nodded his head at her, and he thought she nodded back. Many of the women were openly weeping to see their men and boys march off for who knew how long, and Gib wanted to believe that Masie had tears in her eyes for him.

Lil' Gib marched away to Camp Dennison with the men and boys of Port William, drumming all the way.

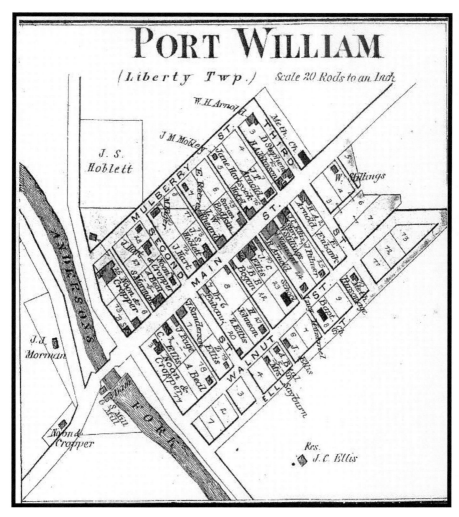

Map of Port William from the 1876 Atlas of Clinton County, Ohio

Chapter Three

Camp Dennison

Gib awoke early, listening to the snores of the men all around him in the camp. It was quite musical really. Some men snored in bass, and others in whistles and lip flapping. Somewhere outside, a sparrow sang two notes slowly, followed by two quick notes. Gib thought he could almost set the sounds to a drum beat. He could smell the acrid campfire of an early riser, and presently came the light of day, though it was still short of full sunrise.

"But when are we going to drill?" asked Gib at breakfast. They had been at Camp Dennison for a week already.

"What do you think we've been doing?" his father replied. "Drill means train. That's what we've been doing all this time."

Gib realized his mistake. He'd thought "drill" meant to drill a hole in a line of Rebels. He was ready to see some action. Since the 79th Ohio Volunteers had been at Camp Dennison, the routine had been pretty much the same each day. Gib was up at 7 a.m. with breakfast at 7:30. Then came guard mounting at 8:30, squad drill at 9, and company drill at 11. Dinner was served at 12:30, followed by more drills, with a dress parade at 5. Gib's drum beat out the calls to these activities. Supper was at 5:30, roll call at 8:30, tattoo at 9, and taps at 10.

When he was not drilling, Gib's detail was to carry water for the men and feed and water the officers' horses, an activity Gib enjoyed. He loved the sound of the soft whickering that the horses made when they saw him coming with their grain. He loved to smooth his hand over the animals' silky manes. Why,

Gib even loved the way the animals smelled when he rested his head upon their warm chests as they drank the cool water Gib poured into the troughs for them. Gib promised himself that he would have his own horse one day.

In the evenings, the recruits sometimes roasted ears of yellow corn in the fragrant campfires while they were entertained by the singing of the choir. And at night, Gib slept in his father's tent. In nearby tents slept two of his uncles and his cousins and friends from Port William. Sometimes Gib thought Camp Dennison was more like a camping trip than an army camp. Why, except for the drilling, he was having fun!

"You'll need to go back to your mother soon, Gib," said John VanZandt when the training was almost done.

"I'm going with you!" Gib insisted.

"Your mother will think I stole you from her if you don't go home," said his father.

But Gib was determined to be a soldier. He might still be a boy in age, but he would show them he could be a man in courage. He wanted to do his part to save the Union!

August 6, 1864
Enlisted as drummer in Company D, 79th Ohio Infantry
Gilbert VanZandt, age ten years, seven months, 16 days old

There was much to learn about drumming for the Union army. Gib took turns beating out the camp calls with other boys who had enlisted as drummers and were training at Camp Dennison. Most of the drummers were teenagers, Gib thought, but he had a hard time telling some people's age. He could tell if someone was his age or if he was really old, like his father or uncles, but anyone's age in between was a mystery to him. What did age matter anyway, thought Gib. It was just a number.

One of the other drummers, a tall red-headed boy named Thomas, was detailed to teach Gib and the others the special drum beats and patterns that made up the battle calls of the army. Thomas was a tease, however, and Gib didn't much like him. One morning when Gib overslept, Thomas told him that the army regularly shot soldiers who slept when they were supposed to be on duty. Gib was some relieved when he found that his punishment for oversleeping was to be a day confined to his tent. Embarrassed, Gib vowed he would never oversleep again.

"A squeak like you won't last long in this army," said Thomas the next day as he looked Gib up and down.

"Don't need long legs to beat the drum," said Gib.

"A baby like you should be home with your mama," Thomas replied and then he began the lesson. Gib had a whole day of learning to make up for.

"These are the calls for camp and training," explained Thomas as he beat out reveille, stable call, breakfast call, sick call, drill call. Gib tried out each rhythm and committed them all to memory. There were 15 drum calls for the men in ranks, and more for the skirmishers. Gib learned them all.

"And these are the beats for when the fighting actually begins." Thomas showed Gib 15 different beats for infantry and another 20 for skirmishes.

"How will I ever remember what to beat and when?" asked Gib.

"When the fightin' starts, squeak, you'll be right in the thick of it so's the men'll be able to hear you. The colonel will shout out the orders," explained Thomas. "And the boy carrying the regimental flag—he'll be the one to mark the position. The men'll be counting on you." Gib felt the chill of fear brush over him for the first time since joining the army. He wasn't about to miss the grand adventure, but when the fighting began would he have the courage to go into battle with the rest of the men from Port William? Gib hoped so.

It turned out that there was even more to know about drumming than Gib had thought possible. Gib soon learned to tap, flam, drag and roll with the drumsticks. He learned the difference between common and quick time. And when he wasn't drumming and drilling, Gib was carrying water, tending to the horses and gathering wood and cooking. Gib didn't mind the hard work because he was with his friends and family—the men of the 79th Ohio Volunteers! But he was anxious to get to the business of fighting, and it seemed to him that they were ready and they'd had enough of drills and details.

One evening after taps, Gib scratched his head and pulled a big louse out of his hair and pinched it between his fingers. All of the recruits in Camp Dennison were plagued by the body lice they called "gray backs." No amount of washing could rid a body of the vermin. Gib sighed and said to his father, "Tonight I'm gonna catch me two gray backs and name them Drill, and Detail. Then I'm going to step on them old gray backs and that'll be the end of drill and detail!" Gib was anxious to get to the real business of the war—saving the Union.

Gib was issued a blue wool coat with brass buttons stamped with a U. S. eagle, but the coat was too large for him. He had to roll up the sleeves when he was drumming. He decided that he would ask his mother to make him a uniform that was his size. His wool trousers could be shortened, but the waist was so big, he had to hold up the trousers with a pair of his father's suspenders.

The 79th Ohio Volunteer Infantry was commanded by Colonel H. G. Kennett of Cincinnati. The Lieutenant Colonel was a Xenia lawyer named Azariah Doan. The boys called Lieutenant Colonel Doan "Pap," because of his kindly ways and because he was a Quaker.

"Quakers don't believe in using titles," his father explained. "They think everyone is the same in God's eyes and ought to be treated that way."

"Why doesn't Pap carry a gun like the other soldiers?" Gib asked his father.

"Quakers don't believe in killing, neither," John VanZandt replied.

"Then why is he a soldier? Isn't that what soldiers do?" asked Gib.

"Pap believes that slavery is wrong and thinks this is the fight to end it," said his father. Until then Gib had thought the war was all about saving the Union. Gib knew about slavery, of course, but since there were no slaves in Port William, he really hadn't given slavery much thought until now. Why, Gib had never even laid eyes on a black person, slave or free. But Gib believed that it could not be right that one man could own another, so here was yet another reason to end the war quickly, he thought.

On the third day of September, 1862, the 79th Ohio received its marching orders.

"We're headin' south to meet the enemy in Kentucky," Thomas said to Gib as they prepared for the long march. "Stay alert and watch out for snipers." Gib thought a sniper must be some kind of snake and he determined to tread carefully as he marched along the road. He didn't suppose a Kentucky snake was any different from an Ohio snake, but who could tell.

"A sniper's prime target is a drummer or flag bearer, cause in the battle they're the ones that keep our boys together. Lose a drummer or a flag bearer in a battle and all hell breaks loose," said Thomas. Gib had not known that he would have such a dangerous role in bringing the war to a close, but he decided then and there he would do whatever he had to do.

Gib had observed that people usually treat you the way you act. Act brave and people will think you are brave, no matter how big or small you might be, Gib thought.

"And take care not to fall behind in the march, squeak. Scalawag Rebels seize stragglers and cut their throats. Then they leave the bodies in the road to warn the next Union soldiers that come marching through," said Thomas.

The march to Louisville proved difficult in a way that Gib had not imagined. The regulation stride of the marching men was a 28-inch step. Gib stood at three and a half feet, and he appeared to be splitting in two as he tried to keep up with the others. Sometimes he had to run to keep up. Gib carried most of his gear in his knapsack, but his drum was an additional weight for Gib's small frame. Inside the drum, Gib stored his special keepsakes, the coin that Lieutenant Ellwood had given him, the buckeye his sister Anna had given him before he left Port William, and some stationery and letters from home. More than once Gib thought about tossing some of his belongings on the roadside just to lighten his load.

Finally, the army crossed the Ohio River at Cincinnati, into Kentucky. Now that they were in enemy country, the order was given to march double quick, and soon Gib fell behind. As Gib struggled to catch up with the others, Lieutenant Colonel Doan rode up beside him on his fine gray mare.

"Give me your hand boy and thee can share my ride for a while," said Lieutenant Colonel Doan, reaching a hand down to Gib. Gratefully, Gib grasped it and the officer pulled Gib up behind him on the horse.

"I'm grateful, sir," said Gib.

"Your Pa asked me to talk to you. Fighting is about to begin. You should go home to your mother, son," said Lieutenant Colonel Doan.

"I'd rather stay in the army, sir, and help save the Union. I want to fight for the flag," said Gib, and then he added, "and I want to fight to throw off slavery. It's my fate," he added with conviction.

"You'd best remember there's two paths to a fate, son. The one thee chooses—and the one thee allows to choose thee," said Lieutenant Colonel Doan. But Gib was determined to stay with the army, and he was ready for adventure. He didn't want to go home anytime soon.

The next evening, tired as he was, Gib took a pen and paper from his drum, and using his drum top as a writing board, he wrote:

Dear Mother

I write to thank you for the uniform that you made for me to wear at the recruiting rallies. I am with father and we are both

very well. Father has asked that I write you this letter so that you would know of my intent. He and Lieutenant Colonel Doan have tried their best to convince me to go home to Port William to finish my schooling, but I feel that my place is here with the army. I know that you both thought that I would grow tired of soldiering drills, but that has not happened. If anything, the camp life has made me even more sure that I want to be a soldier. My commanding officer has offered to make a special request to the War Department for me to be OFFICIALLY mustered into the army so that I might draw pay as any other soldier. Please give my love to Anna and little Will. Know that I love you truly, and that I will soon be home once we've whupped the Rebels and saved the Union!
Your loving son,
Gib

P.S. I will be able to visit you for two weeks' furlough in a few months. But make no mistake, if the war is still going on then, I shall return to the army.

The troops crossing the Ohio River from Cincinnati, Ohio to Kentucky. (Harper's Pictorial History of the Civil War)

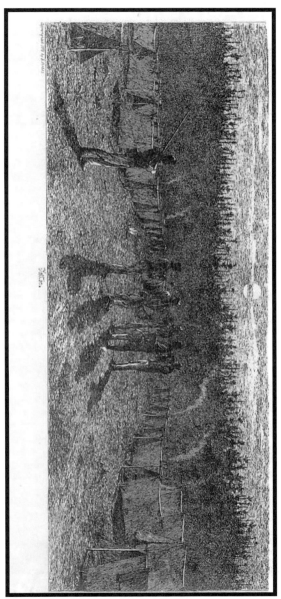

Drummer boys beating out tattoo in camp, sketched by Edwin Forbes. (Dover Pictorial Archives)

Lil Gib's military records showing his official muster-in date of Oct. 31, 1862 at age 10.

Chapter Four

Billy and Banjo

"Name's William Baner. Friends call me Billy," said the boy.

"Gib VanZandt; pleased to meet you," said Gib, recognizing Billy as Lieutenant Colonel Doan's new orderly. Billy was a wiry fellow with laughing blue eyes and blonde hair. Billy's nose was peeling from recent sunburn, and he had just a shadow of a moustache on his upper lip. Billy was leading the beautiful gray mare that was Lieutenant Colonel Doan's favorite mount. Gib reached out and stroked the mare's soft muzzle, and the beautiful horse nickered and nuzzled Gib's hand looking for a treat.

"This here is Betsy," said Billy, not knowing that it was Gib who had taken care of the animal while they were at Camp Dennison. Gib took a piece of hardtack from his pocket and offered it to the mare. She sniffed and turned away. Gib and Billy chuckled. Everyone knew, even horses apparently, that the hard crackers had to be soaked for a spell before you could eat them.

"I actually bit into a hardtack once and durn'd if it wasn't soft," said Billy.

"A worm?" asked Gib. Hardtack was often infested with worms.

"Nope. A nail," said Billy.

Gib chuckled at the joke, and stroked Betsy's mane.

"I look after the horses for Pap. He says we can ride Betsy together when we march out of Louisville. Then he says we'll look for a smaller horse or maybe a pony for you to ride," said Billy. Gib was thrilled. A horse of his own!

Just then, a scruffy terrier came bounding up to the boys, barking, its tail wagging. The dog sat down and looked adoringly at Billy, its tail beating a perfect tattoo on the ground. Billy knelt and the animal hurtled into his arms. "This here is my dog Banjo. He followed me to war," said Billy. Lots of the soldiers had pets. One man had a squirrel named Bun that sat on his shoulder eating hardtack. A Wisconsin regiment had an eagle named Old Abe, and, another, a screech owl named Minerva. The columns swarmed with dogs, and one soldier had a pet bear.

Over the next few days, Gib and Billy became good friends as they rode together on Betsy, with Banjo at their heels. The two boys and the dog were inseparable. One day, Billy and Gib and Banjo were strolling through the camp when Thomas approached them.

"Used to have a dog just like that at home. Give you a month's pay for that mutt," Thomas offered. Gib was astonished when Billy agreed.

"Only on the condition that you never tie him up," said Billy.

"Deal," said Thomas.

"You can't sell Banjo!" Gib protested. But Billy pocketed the money and strode off, Gib following. Thomas picked up a whimpering Banjo and carried him into his tent.

"He can't keep that dog in there forever, and when he lets Banjo out, the cur'll find me, mark my words," said Billy, chuckling. Why I sold that dog two, three times already, but he always finds his way back to me sooner or later." Sure enough, by the next morning Banjo had found his way back to Billy.

Soon, Billy began to draw Gib into his pranks. In camp, a few tents had been fitted with chimneys made of dirt and sticks for the fireplaces within. The choir tent had such a chimney. And in this tent the choir practiced their songs every evening before taps.

One evening, Billy and Gib sat with Banjo near a campfire listening to the choir, and Billy said, "Let's go have us some fun."

"What are you meaning to do?" asked Gib.

Billy grabbed a pail of water from beside the smoldering campfire outside the choir tent and handed it to Gib. He gave Banjo a command to stay by the fire, and the dog obeyed.

"I'm going to boost you up, and when I say 'now' you throw the water down the chimney."

Gib was unsure. He set the pail back down on the ground.

"Come on sport. No one will get hurt and we'll have us a good laugh," urged Billy.

Billy boosted Gib upon his shoulders and handed him the bucket. The choir sang on, and when they came to the verse, "Scotland's burning, cast on water," Billy said, "Now!" Gib hoisted up the bucket and poured the water down the chimney.

Inside, the choir stopped singing abruptly as the tent filled with smoke, and the choking men rushed outside to find the pranksters. But by then, Gib and Billy, with Banjo right behind them, had run for cover into the woods around the camp where they collapsed in laughter.

The boys' friendship deepened as the weeks went by. It seemed to Gib that Billy had enough stories to fill a book, but Gib could never tell if Billy was telling the truth or pulling his leg. One night after they were finished with feeding and watering the horses, the boys walked together back through the field to the camp. It was a warm night, and the lightening bugs were making pinpricks of light against the darkness. Gib caught one of the insects and held it in his cupped hands so that it could not fly away. The insect flashed light from the opening between his hands.

"Back home in Xenia, my brothers and I kept a pet frog in a box under our bed. Every evening, that old bullfrog would croak up a storm. Bout drove Ma crazy trying to find what was making all the noise. We used to collect lightening bugs in a jar and feed them to that old bull frog and his throat would glow all night." Gib didn't know what to make of Billy's story, but he rather doubted it. He opened his hands and let the insect fly off to join its friends in the night.

Gib was sure Billy was lying when Billy announced the next day "General Nelson's been killed. Murdered!" But, suddenly, other men in the camp were shouting the news that General Nelson was dead.

"Was it the Rebs?" Gib asked, thinking that perhaps a sharpshooter had picked off the General. Since they had been in Louisville, the regiment reported to General William Nelson. Thus far, the 79th Ohio had seen little fighting except for a few skirmishes from Confederate guerillas, but sharpshooters were a constant threat.

"Naw. He was shot by one of our own. General Davis shot him. They had a falling out in camp, and General Davis drew his gun and killed General Nelson with a single shot."

This time, Gib discovered, Billy really was telling the truth. Gib had heard all about General Davis from his father, who had recently been promoted to Sergeant.

"General Davis fired the first shot at Fort Sumter in SC where this whole war began, or so he claims," said Gib. They say he has a bad temper—all the boys are afraid of him."

In the next few days, Gib and Billy learned a great deal more about General Davis, who miraculously was not charged for the murder of his fellow officer.

"General Davis is all about saving the Union, but he doesn't much care if slavery ends," said Billy.

"I thought all Union soldiers were fighting to free the slaves," Gib said.

"Naw. General Davis is a pro slavery Indianan," said Billy, but Gib wondered if Billy was telling the truth about that. Gib could understand why some southerners could be against slavery, but he didn't believe that any northerner would be for it.

Three days later, the 79th Ohio, including Gib and Billy attended the funeral of General Nelson. Gib beat on his drum with one stick as the funeral procession marched through the camp.

The army was ordered to Frankfort and then to Bowling-Green. Sometimes Gib marched with the other drummers, but more often than not he rode with Col Doan or Billy astride Betsy. As the army went further into Rebel territory, the men and boys of the 79th Ohio began to see signs of great struggles. Until now, they had only been engaged in minor skirmishes resulting in little bloodshed. But now, signs of the enemy were all around.

One evening, Gib saw for the first time a man who had been wounded in a skirmish. The wounded man had been brought into camp, his clothing covered with blood, his face pale. Gib followed when the man was taken to the surgeon. He felt a cold chill run through him when he looked at the medical tools laid out on the surgeon's table.

"Do you want me to give you anything before the operation?" the surgeon asked. The man had been shot in the shoulder.

"Wouldn't mind a glass of liquor before you commence cuttin'," said the soldier. The surgeon gave him the drink. Then he took a knife and began to cut away the torn shirt, and with the same knife trimmed away the torn and bleeding flesh of the wound. An attack of dizziness made Gib's head swim and he felt sick to his stomach. He turned away from the spectacle, but he would never forget the look of pain and fear on the wounded soldier's face.

The army marched south through the cold and drizzle, catching rain water to drink because the Rebels had poisoned the springs and creeks by throwing in the bodies of rotting animals. Some of the thirsty soldiers drank the water anyway, and they became very sick. Often the roads were churned into mud by the men and horses that passed on ahead of them, and they had to stop and corduroy the roads with logs so that the men and horses could get a footing and the artillery could be rolled over the solid surface. Gib began to think that war was more about marching than about fighting.

After a few days' rest, the regiment marched to Scottsville and then to Gallatin, Tennessee, where they made camp. Altogether they had marched nearly 500 miles, so they were glad for a rest. While Gib and Billy were helping make camp and tending the horses, Thomas approached them. He was still fuming over the double cross that Banjo had pulled.

"Hey, squeak," said Thomas. The red-headed boy dropped to his knees and walked around a bit in imitation of Gib's gait.

"Well, squeak, don't know as I like being this close to the ground," he teased. "I can see now why you like to ride Pap's horse instead of splitting yourself in two on the march. Maybe the Colonel can find a Rebel mule for you to ride," said Thomas. He was grinning but he looked worn out from the march, and his face was splotchy.

"Haven't seen any mules in camp, but I think I know where there's a jackass," said Billy, stepping between Gib and Thomas protectively. Gib stepped out from behind his friend. He could take care of his own self. Besides, he knew that Thomas was just joking, though he wasn't a bit funny.

"Maybe my legs are too short to keep up with the double quick, but once the fighting's started, you'll see what makes me a soldier!" said Gib. Billy stepped up closer to Thomas and looked him full in the face.

"What's the matter with your face Thomas? It looks like an army of gray backs marched across it," said Billy. Gib saw that angry red spots covered the drummer's face.

"Better get yourself to the infirmary Thomas. I think you have the pox. Could be contagious," said Billy and he grabbed Gib's arm and backpedaled away from Thomas.

The red spots on Thomas's face turned out to be measles, which rapidly spread through the camp. Many of the boys died. Their bodies, weakened from the long hard march and poor food, were not able to throw off the sickness. A few days later, Billy also sickened and was taken to the infirmary tent that smelled of vomit and was crowded with more than 100 sick soldiers. The men lay on the hard ground with only half dozen or so blankets to share among themselves. The surgeon ordered bed rest and quinine, but he could do little else to ease their suffering. Gib, who managed to escape the disease, thought he would rather die in battle than of measles. When it was over, many of the sick had indeed perished, including Thomas.

Much to Gib's relief, Billy Baner recovered

Chapter Five

"It hain't hurt me yet"

Colonel Henry Kennett, commander of the 79th Ohio, regarded the small boy who stood in front of him. Gib had dressed in the uniform his mother made for him—a blue wool coat with brass buttons, and gray pants held up with suspenders. He had polished the fine shoes his father had made for him before they left Port William, though now their soles were thin from the long march.

"Sir, I wish to apply for a musket so that I might be a soldier when the battle begins," said Gib. "We've lost many soldiers to the measles. Perhaps I might be issued one of their muskets."

"But you are a drummer. Besides, army regulations do not permit anyone under the age of 18 to carry a gun," said Colonel Kennett.

"Then I should need a sword," said Gib, eyeing the Colonel's saber that hung by his side. The Colonel drew out the saber and stood its point on the ground beside Gib. The hilt of the weapon reached the top of Gib's kepi.

Actual letter written Aug 1, 1863, from Gilbert VanZandt of the 79th Ohio to editor of The Clinton Republican, published in Wilmington, Ohio, on August 14, 1863, to mark Gilbert VanZandt's one year anniversary with the army.

Lavergne, Tenn.
August 1st, 1863

Mr. Editor,

Dear Sir—*Thinking a few lines from me, perhaps, would interest you a little, I send these to you. Well, a little past ten years old, I, with my father and friends, on the 9th of last August entered Camp Dennison; and how proud I felt with my little drum on my back a-going in the army as a drummer boy, and be with the brave soldiers who had started out to defend our country. I was willing to leave my dear mother and my little brother and sister, and my little soft bed, and my mother's table, and my little friends and school mates, and pleasant home, to go in the army as a drummer boy, to share all of the hardships and dangers and exposure of the soldier's life; which I have done thus far with pleasure. I have been in the army almost one year now, and have spent the time and enjoyed myself bravely. I like to be a soldier, although we have seen some hard times; but I did not get home sick. I have not been home sick since I first came in the army; but I was glad to see my dear mother and sister once more; and after a visit of two weeks I again returned to the Regiment, and was glad to see my father and the rest of the soldiers, and my much esteemed friend Colonel Doan (Lieutenant Colonel Azariah Doan), and the rest of the officers, who are good and kind to me.*

I have many kind friends in the Regiment, whom I never shall forget, long after the war is over and we are separated; and, won't never forget the Colonel (Henry G.) Kennett for the kindness he has shown to me, and the little sword that he presented to me as a token of his love and respect. And this little sword I will take home with me when the war is over, and look at it and think of the giver with love and respect, and remember where I was when I received it, away down in Tennessee, about four hundred miles from my home, a little drummer boy in the great army of the Union. And how often I have looked at our beautiful flag, as it was borne along on some of our long marches in the sturdy hands of some of its defenders. I say how often I have looked at it, and asked God to bless it, and forbid that it should ever be destroyed. And oh how nice it flutters in the air when we are on battalion drill, and dress parade, when all of the soldiers are fixed up with their "rig, all bright and clean and their white glove on.

I have seen a great many things, and been in a great many towns, and seen some rebs, and didn't like the looks of them. I have had good health all the time, better than I ever had at home; and sometimes had nothing to eat but hard crackers and fat meat, and black coffee, but I thought if the rest could live on it I could, so it was all right with me. And we have slept out on the ground in the rain and mud, and in the cold and warm, wet and dry. I expect some of my little friends would think that such usage would kill them, and you may think it too hard for a little boy like me, but it hain't hurt me yet and I hope to keep in good health until I can beat the death-knell of the Southern Confederacy on my little drum. It was bright and new when I first came out, but now it looks quite old from the service in the army; but it sounds as well as ever yet.

Our Regiment is in good health and fine spirits, but we have had a good many to die; and how sad I felt beating the dead march going to their graves; and the mournful tune of the fife and the doleful sound of our drums created feelings that none but the soldier knows, following a comrade to his grave. These things I can never forget, but will ever remember them, that I, with the rest of the drummers beat the dead march as we marched to their last resting place. But we think that it won't be long now until the war will be over, then I will throw my drum over my shoulder and return with my father and friends to my home in Port William. But I don't expect to go home anymore until the war is over, for I am too far from home now. We are down in Dixey and I can play the tune of Dixey on my drum pretty well, and I shall remember Dixey's land whenever I play the tune on my drum. But I like to be a soldier and will see the end of the war if I live, before I come home and leave the army. Then, perhaps, you can see me in Wilmington on my way home.

Gilbert VanZandt
Drummer boy in Co. D, 79th Reg. O. V. I.

But Gib knew that even though he might live to return to the place of his birth, he would never be able to return to his boyhood. Too much had happened. Too much had changed.

Drummer boys off duty playing cards in camp. (Library of Congress)

Chapter Six

Battle of Resaca

Throughout the winter of 1863 and 1864, Gib's regiment was ordered to guard the railroads and supplies in Tennessee. Then in March they moved over the Cumberland Mountains into Georgia. In the reorganization of the army, they were now part of General Sherman's army. Like the men and boys of Port William, Sherman was also an Ohioan, and his soldiers, who loved him, called him "Uncle Billy."

Gib didn't know exactly where they were going, but he knew they were on the way to something big. They slept in the open air at the end of each day's long march. They ate whatever they could forage from farms and towns along their route.

"General Sherman's aim is to capture Atlanta," said Gib's father. "The Rebs will do all they can to stop us." Gib was still bunking with his father at night after he finished beating out the camp calls on his drum.

"We've orders to destroy the city's railroads and factories-- that'll bring this war to a swift close for sure," said Sergeant VanZandt.

"I'd say we're about to see the elephant," said Gib. Billy had told him that to see the elephant meant to come face to face with the enemy, but Gib never knew when to believe Billy. Gib's father didn't correct him, though, so Billy must have been telling the truth.

The next day Gib's father came to him and held out a letter. His expression was solemn. At first Gib thought that something must have happed to his mother or to Anna or baby Will. Gib unfolded the pages and read.

Dear John and Gilbert,

I have received news this very day that my brother Zachariah has been captured and is being held in Libby Prison. I have sent off a letter to the Army asking for the particulars. In the meantime, I must put the best face on capture, and am grateful that it is a capture rather than a minie ball that's found Zach. The news comes from another soldier who was with Zach when they went out to scout. A third man was killed outright, and the soldier who wrote me the news was able to escape and hid out. He thought Zach must be alright cause he heard him cursing the Rebs so bad, and then he heard the Rebs say they'd be taking Zach to Richmond, and then they'd see who was going to hell. As dire as that seems we must put the best face on it, for at least we know Zach is alive. Because he was on scout, he had his bedroll and some food and dishes with him, and his pocket Bible our Mother gave him so perhaps he will make out fine in prison. What are they saying about Libby anyway?

Your loving wife and mother,
Nancy VanZandt

    Now, Gib thought grimly, there was one more reason to get the war over with quickly. And soon, the order was given to march. At first Gib marched along on foot with the other drummers, but when the order was given to march "double quick time" Gib rode with Lieutenant Colonel Doan on Betsy. When Betsy tired, Lieutenant Colonel Doan walked beside them as Gib alone rode Betsy.
    Gib had still not seen a live battle, but he had seen the aftermath of some terrible struggles. Their route had led through the Chicamauga Valley, where a great battle had taken place the

previous September. Gib had never believed in ghosts, but if a place could be haunted, then that battlefield surely was. It seemed to Gib as though the ghosts of hundreds of dead soldiers—both Yankees and Rebels—were still battling on that ground.

The fields and woods gleamed in the moonlight reflected off the bleached bones of dead soldiers from both sides. Many of the fallen seemed to have never been buried at all, and others had been covered only partially. Beside one country road, Gib had seen a skeleton hand reaching up from out of the ground, its fingers splayed as though it were waving at him. He quickly looked away.

Shortly, all the talk was about the big battle ahead. The troops were jumpy and alert while on the march, and when they made camp at night, they spent their precious free time cleaning their weapons and preparing for the fight to come. In mid May, they were ordered to assault the enemy at a place called Resaca. Gib was assigned to beat the drum calls in the field.

As they awaited for the call to march forward, Gib looked around him. It seemed so peaceful here, so serene in the Georgia landscape. The men were uncharacteristically quiet. There was no sound except for the rustling of the leaves in the warm breeze and the music of the birds. Billy stood next to Gib, nervous with anticipation. Banjo had been tied up in camp where he would be safe from Rebel sharpshooters.

"They say that before a battle, the Rebel officers give their soldiers whiskey mixed with gun powder. It makes them furious and they fight like hell," whispered Billy.

"I don't believe it," said Gib. He was getting better at being able to tell when Billy was fibbing or not.

Suddenly an eerie wail pierced the crisp morning air. At first, Gib thought it must be an animal. He had heard a similar sound once before on an early spring day in Port William when he and his mother had been walking near the pond on his uncle's farm—a long, haunting wail that Gib had never forgotten.

"That's the cry of a loon," Gib's mother had said. She pointed out the big black and white bird that Gib might have mistaken for a duck or a goose except for its long beak.

"It must be hurt dreadful to make a sound like that" Gib had said.

"No, that's just the sound a loon makes. Must be on its way back north and stopped here to rest. Don't often see nor hear loons here in Ohio," she said. Gib had counted himself lucky to have heard the cry of a loon on that day that seemed so long ago.

The sound Gib heard now was equally disturbing—high pitched, tremulous. It made the hair stand up on the back of his neck.

"That's the Rebel yell," whispered Billy.

Winter found Gib's blood. Gib knew that he would never forget that sound, but unlike the cry of the loon, he would never want to remember it.

The command came. "Onward! Forward! Double Quick!" Gib began to beat on his drum.

Suddenly there was confusion everywhere. Minie balls flew through the air all around him, but Gib kept drumming. The men were loading and firing as fast as they could, tearing paper cartridges with their teeth as the Confederates kept coming at them. A shell burst near him, and through the woods in the direction of the firing, he saw a long line of men dressed in gray, moving forward towards them. In the times when the breeze cleared the smoke, Gib could see beyond the line of Rebs straight ahead of him where a line of artillery was getting ready to fire. Still, Gib kept drumming, but he thought in his fright that the whole Rebel army must be aiming for him. His knees shook violently and he felt cold, even as the heat of the battle raged around him.

And then the lines of blue soldiers, among them his father and uncles and cousins and all his friends from Port William, were around him yelling and firing, and he watched, still drumming out the calls, as some of them were wounded and fell to the ground. He could no longer hear the rhythm of his drum over the awesome roar of cannons and the thunk of shells as they hit the trees and the sound of cracking bones and the screams of men, some of whom he had known his whole life in Port William, Ohio. But even then he kept drumming.

In the midst of the confusion all around him, Gib saw a man whose arm had been cut off by a round shot, as clean and smooth as if it had been severed by a surgeon's knife. Bravely, the man made a tourniquet and tied it off with his good hand and his teeth to stop the bleeding. Then the wounded man calmly walked to the rear.

Gib saw another soldier hit in the leg, but the wounded man kept moving forward. A bullet tore open the man's chest, but he still didn't stop. When he got to the top of the hill, the soldier toppled and bled to death while the fighting went on around him. Gib looked around him and saw the familiar flag of the Twentieth Army Corps. Frantically, he searched the faces of the men fighting near him for a glimpse of his father. He kept drumming. The battle went on until nightfall.

Gib had already seen and heard and felt things in this war he wished he hadn't. He had smelled the stench of rotting flesh and the sickening odor of unwashed men as they lay dying from disease. He had endured unbearable heat and cold on the long marches. He had been so hungry that a wormy hardtack cracker tasted as sweet as his mother's apple pie. But of all the horrors that Gib had experienced of war, what he thought he would remember most was the sound of the Rebel yell.

When the battle was over, it seemed as if the entire Confederate army still stood in their way. They were headed for Atlanta, said Colonel Doan. Sherman had vowed to make Georgia howl.

Shelling of the railroad near Resaca, sketched by Edwin Forbes. (Dover Pictorial Archives)

Chapter Seven

Fighting at Kennesaw Mountain

*"Future years will never know
the seething hell and black infernal background,
and it is best they should not."*
—**Walt Whitman**

"I've a new assignment for thee, my young man," said Colonel Doan to Gib a few days after the fighting at Resaca ended. "General Ward is needing a new orderly, and I believe thee is the man for the job."

"He was glad the Colonel called him a man instead of boy or son." Gib felt he deserved it. He had never flinched during the Battle of Resaca, though death and injury were all around him. He had proven that he could be as brave as any soldier twice his age. And now he was to be made an orderly!

"I'll do whatever I'm ordered, no matter what," replied Gib.

Colonel Doan put a hand on Gib's shoulder. "Remember, duty may be ours but the consequences are God's," he said. "Now, report to General Ward!"

"Yes sir!" said Gib, and he wasted no time making his way to headquarters.

Although Gib would miss making camp with his Port William regiment, life at headquarters would be more interesting. If there were more battles to come, Gib thought he would be better able to take part in them as a dispatch carrier than as a drummer. And besides, as a dispatch carrier, he would be able to spend more time with his pal Billy.

General Ward, a Kentuckian who was said to be fond of whiskey and fine horses, looked skeptical when he saw the little boy who had been sent to him as an orderly.

"You could be called to deliver messages at any hour—in camp or in battle. When you're not needed for dispatches, then you'll be out foraging. Think you can handle this job, boy?" asked General Ward.

"I can do it sir!" said Gib.

"Then this'll be your mount. She's the smallest we have, though probably a bit too big for you. Her name's Susie," said General Ward after they had walked to the horse pens. Gen Ward pointed out a small chestnut mare. Gib thought he had never seen a finer horse--finally, a horse of his own.

"Thank you, sir. I'll take good care of her," said Gib. Gib knew that seeing was louder than talking. He'd show General Ward what a good dispatch carrier he could be. But Gib knew that he was too small to mount the horse by himself. He would have to ask Billy to lift him upon the mare.

By mid June Sherman's army, including the 79th Ohio and Gib, were approaching Kennesaw Mountain. At first, they made some headway overrunning Confederate pickets north of the enemy. Then, on the morning of June 27, Sherman sent his troops forward over the Burnt Hickory Road, but found that attacking an enemy that was firmly dug in was futile. During the worst of the fighting, General Ward summoned Gib.

"I want you to take Susie and deliver this dispatch to Lieutenant Harryman as fast as you can," he ordered. Quickly, Gib saddled Susie, and using a milk stool borrowed from the camp cook, mounted the little horse and rode off.

As he rode toward the sound of the battle, Gib worried that he would not be able to find Lieutenant Harryman in the confusion of the fighting. Gib leaned low over Susie's back to make himself less of a target and urged Susie off in the direction he had last seen Lieutenant Harryman. Gib and Susie rode fast through a small clearing surrounded by a split rail fence.

The field was dotted with bright, yellow dandelions. At home in Port William, Gib had called the flowers wishweeds. He would close his eyes and make a wish and then blow the fuzzy seeds, scattering them over the field behind his house. Now he barely saw the flowers as Susie trampled over them.

Suddenly Gib felt a breeze on his cheek as a minie ball flew by him and then he heard the shot. Quickly, Gib urged Susie toward the shelter of the trees where they stopped to take cover. While they rested, Gib looked in the direction of the fighting and saw that a soldier in blue was crawling on his hands and knees along the line of the fence, where he dropped to the ground face down and rolled close to the bottom rail of the fence. Gib wondered if the soldier had been shot, but then the soldier moved and began to crawl away from the direction of the fighting. The soldier was lying as close to the fence rails as possible, as if the wood would offer some protection from the flying minie balls and grape shot that whizzed around him.

Then Gib saw Lieutenant Harryman, who came along on his horse. The officer seemed to spot the cowering soldier because suddenly Lieutenant Harryman veered off toward the fence and drew his sword. Was Lieutenant Harryman going to kill his own man, Gib wondered. Gib watched Lieutenant Harryman give the man a good dubbing with the flat side of the sword blade and then point to the front, as if ordering the soldier back into battle. The soldier rose and shambled off toward the front. Before Lieutenant Harryman could ride away, Gib rode up to him and delivered the dispatch.

"Did you see that coward, son? Thinking he could hide behind a fence rail and leave the fighting to everyone else!" Lieutenant Harryman exclaimed--his face red with anger, and Gib saw that his shirt was spattered with blood. Was it his own or the blood of another wounded soul?

Gib wondered if the man would be court martialed after the battle—if he survived it, that is. One time near Resaca, Colonel Doan had caught two enlisted men running away from the battle instead of toward it. The men had been arrested after the battle was over, and then drummed out of camp. Gib himself had beat out the rhythm to "Rogue's March" as the men were escorted out. First, they were stripped of their uniforms and equipment, and the men were marched through the camp, with a guard on either side and four soldiers following, and the fife and drum corps bringing up the rear. The others hooted and jeered as the two shamed soldiers were marched the entire length of the camp.

But unlike those two, the soldier by the fence rail had returned to the thick of the battle. Gib wondered if this man was a coward for trying to hide. Or was he courageous for returning to battle in spite of his terror? What was bravery anyway, Gib wondered. After Resaca, an officer had asked his staff to define bravery.

"Fearlessness," said the General.

"Madness," said Pap Doan.

"Stupidity," said a private.

The dead piled high on the mountainside. And then, the fighting ended with the firing of three rifle volleys that meant both sides could clear the battlefield of dead and wounded. Soldiers from both sides worked side by side, using boards from hardtack boxes as headstones for their fallen comrades. When that grim task was complete, each side would fire three more volleys to signal that the killing and wounding could resume. Among the Union dead was Ohio's Colonel Daniel McCook, the fourth member of his family to be killed in action.

When the fighting finally ended, Gib was ordered to help retrieve the Union wounded and dead from the battlefield. Now, here he sat in a battlefield that stank of blood and fear and excrement and unwashed soldiers. Among the living, fear and despair hung over the field thicker than the acrid smoke of the cannons and guns. Gib wondered why he had ever imagined that the business of war would be glorious adventure. Grown men were calling for their mamas. The drone of the blowflies was endless. Gib moved among the wounded, giving them water and assurance that ambulances would soon come to carry them off the field. Gib recognized several Port William men among the dead, and he hoped his father was not among them. He thought also of his uncles and cousins. And he thought of Billy Baner, whom he had not seen since the fighting began.

Union and Rebel soldiers lay on the battlefield side by side. Gib walked through the field looking for signs of life. One dead Rebel soldier stared up at him with lifeless eyes. He looked not much older than Gib, and Gib saw that the boy wasn't wearing shoes. His feet were dirty and calloused as if he had never worn shoes. In his fist, the dead soldier clutched the straps of a knapsack. Without loosening the straps from the soldier's grip, Gib opened the knapsack and pulled out a pair of shoes—small, possibly made for a child about a year or so old, his brother Will's age. The shoes were very crudely made out of beaten leather, perhaps from the leather salvaged from an old pair of the dead Rebel's own shoes, Gib thought. Maybe that was why the soldier was barefoot. Gib wondered if the baby who lost the shoes might also have lost a father or brother in this brave, dead boy who had fought barefoot. He blinked back tears but even with his eyes shut he could see the criss cross of the tiny shoelaces. Gib first thought it odd that he should be so affected by the sight of those small shoes, but most times, he knew that people were more affected by the little things that happen to themselves than by the big things that happen to others. Gib kept the little shoes. He wanted to show them to his father back in camp, and then he would store them in his drum.

Throughout the evening, Gib moved among the wounded, giving water to the injured men who were lifted onto stretchers and taken to the hospital tent where the surgeons were at work. Outside the tent, Gib saw piles of arms and legs stacked like firewood. Inside the tent, he could hear the screams of the men as the surgeons hacked off their limbs. Right then and there Gib decided it was better to die on the battlefield than to be wounded. He leaned against a tree and threw up.

"You'll get used to it, son. It's just the way of war," said one of the blood soaked surgeons as he emerged from the tent and threw another leg upon the growing pile of limbs.

Get used to it? Gib didn't think so. Maybe as time went on, some things got harder and harder to take. Like frostbite. Gib remembered one winter in Ohio when his fingers had been numbed with cold as he was cutting ice in the stream. At first he lost all feeling in them, but then as the numbness wore off, the pain burned hot. War was like that. It might numb you at first, but Gib didn't think he'd ever get used to the horror of killing and wounding—it would only become more horrible as time went on. For the first time since he'd enlisted, Gib cursed the war and vowed to do anything he could to end it.

"The Rogue's March," photographed by Matthew Brady, shows a soldier being drummed out of camp for thievery. (Library of Congress)

Chapter Eight

Sherman's Bummers

Orders issued by William Sherman concerning foraging:

The army will forage liberally on the country during the march. To this end, each brigade commander will organize a good and sufficient foraging party, under the command of one or more discreet officers, who will gather, near the route traveled, corn or forage of any kind, meat of any kind, vegetables, corn-meal, or whatever is needed by the command, aiming at all times to keep in the wagons at least ten days' provisions for his command, and three days' forage. Soldiers must not enter the dwellings; they may be permitted to gather turnips, potatoes, and other vegetables, and to drive in stock in sight of their camp.

To corps commanders alone is entrusted the power to destroy mills, houses, cotton-gins, etc. and for them the general principle is laid down: In districts and neighborhoods where the army is unmolested, no destruction of such property should be permitted; but should guerillas or bush-whackers molest our march, or should the inhabitants burn bridges, obstruct roads, or otherwise manifest local hostility, then army commanders should order and enforce a devastation more or less relentless, according to the measure of such hostility. As for horses, mules, wagons, etc., belonging to the inhabitants, the cavalry and artillery may appropriate freely and without limit; dis-

criminating, however, between the rich, who are usually hostile, and the poor and industrious, usually neutral or friendly.

"In making your camp fires, never burn any but the top fence rails," ordered Colonel Doan, in keeping with the spirit of General Sherman's orders. A fence could still keep livestock in and protect property with its top rail missing. One day Gib and Billy were sent for firewood, but they found that the top rails had already been removed from all the fencing in the vicinity.

"Did you ever notice that after you burn the top rail, that there's always a rail underneath that then becomes the top rail?" said Billy. It made some sense, Gib had to admit; so, he helped Billy remove the next rail, which they chopped up for firewood.

It seemed Sherman's army was always in short supply, but the Union troops managed to get what they needed, sometimes in very clever ways. One of the nurses of Sherman's army was a stout woman the soldiers called Mother Bickerdyke. She was the only woman that Sherman would allow on the front, but mostly she stayed at the hospitals. In the spring of 1863, when supplies were hard to come by, Mother Bickerdyke's boys, were wanting for food and supplies. She hit upon a plan, and when the medical director came into the hospital one day, she confronted him.

"Doctor, do you know we are paying these Secesh 50 cents for every quart of milk we use—two thirds chalk and water—that if you should pour it into the trough of a respectable pig at home, he would turn up his nose and run off, squealing in disgust?"

"Well, what can we do about it?" asked the doctor.

"If you'll give me 30 days' furlough and transportation, I'll go home and get all the milk and eggs the hospitals can use," she replied.

"Get milk and eggs! Why, you could not bring them down here even if the North would give you all it has. A barrel of eggs would spoil in this warm weather before it could reach us. And how on earth could you bring milk?" asked the doctor.

"Give me furlough and transportation, and let me try it!" she persisted.

The Doctor granted the furlough and Mother B traveled to St. Louis accompanied by several hundred war amputees. She placed these men in hospitals, and then continued on to Chicago where she asked a wealthy farmer to donate 100 cows to the Cause. She also received many hens. Before the furlough ended, Mother B returned to her hospital in Tennessee, forming a long parade that included the cows and hens. Mother B told the southerners that these were "loyal cows and hens; none of your miserable trash that give chalk and water for milk, and lay loud smelling eggs!"

Now that Sherman's army was deep into Georgia, the men often went to the outlying farms to loot and confiscate what they needed. These foragers were called "bummers" by the Confederate civilians who hated them. Gib and Billy often rode out together with Banjo on foraging expeditions, looking for supplies for the army. These expeditions might have been fun excursions except when it became necessary to take food from the farms that dotted the countryside. The Confederate farms were a sorry sight this late in the war, with women, children and old men carrying on the back-breaking work of planting and harvesting without the help of their men folk. Some of the larger farms had slaves, of course, but when President Lincoln had issued the Emancipation Proclamation the previous year, many of the slaves had simply walked away from their owners.

The civilians they met looked tired and worn out. It was as though they'd stopped caring if they won or lost the war, because *anyone* winning or losing was better than having the war go on. War was awful enough for the soldiers, but what about the common folks? They suffered more, it seemed to Gib, losing their homes and their livelihood, and many times their loved ones as well.

One day when Billy and Gib were foraging, they knocked on the door of a farmhouse that had definitely seen better days.

"What you want here, Yanks?" said the teenaged girl who came to the door. Her dress was stained, but her chestnut hair had been brushed shiny.

"We're looking for feed for Sherman's horses," said Gib.

"You boys have already stripped us of everything. We don't even have any horses, so why would we have feed?" she replied.

"Look, here. We didn't start this war," said Billy. The angry tone of his voice made Banjo growl low in his throat.

"Oh really?" she spat back. "Who invited you Yanks down here anyway? Not my Pa, who's layin' dead in Mississippi. Not my Ma, who's sick abed upstairs with no money to buy medicine if some was to be had. Not my brother, who's lost an arm. So you tell me, is this any way to wage a war? Stealing from poor folks like us, who've already lost just about everything?"

"I guess we'll just be taking a look in that barn on yonder to see what we can find anyway, ma'am," said Billy. The girl slammed the door, and Billy and Gib stepped off the porch and headed to the barn, with Banjo scampering on ahead.

"Any grain won't be in plain sight," said Gib, knowing of the farmers' attempt to hide what they could keep from the foragers. Sure enough, Gib and Billy eventually found several sacks of feed which they hoisted over their shoulders and carried to the horses. After securing the sacks of the animals, Gib and Billy headed out of the farmyard towards the road.

Suddenly Gib heard the sharp crack of a rifle and felt a bullet whiz by his ear. Instinctively, he ducked and stole a look at Billy next to him.

"Ride!" Billy exclaimed, and he hunched over his mount and urged his horse to a gallop. Banjo raced along beside them, his ears laid back in fear.

Crack. A second bullet was fired from the house, and Gib wondered if it was the pretty Rebel girl who had answered the door who was firing at them. She hadn't looked like a killer. Crack.

Gib felt Susie shudder and then the mare dropped to her knees. But Gib held on tightly as the horse lifted its head and screamed. Gib scrambled off the mare's back as Susie fell over and lay on the ground, her legs flailing. She lifted her head, her beautiful eyes making an appeal to Gib for help. Blood sprayed from her nostrils. Gib wrapped his arms around the mare's head and buried his face in her sweet smelling hide, and then Gib felt himself being lifted from the ground and tossed over the saddle of Billy's horse. One more shot rang out, and Gib knew Susie was gone.

That evening Gib and Billy rode slowly back towards camp with what little they had been able to forage. Gib rode behind Billy on Billy's horse, and Banjo trotted along beside them. Poor Susie, thought Gib. She had been a good horse and a brave one. Neither boy spoke as they rode along the dusty road, alert for any signs of the enemy. But the only enemy they saw was a bunch of the dead ones. By the side of the road lay five dead Rebel soldiers. Their bodies were still, and flies swarmed around their eyes. It looked as if they had tried to crawl together across the road to reach the shade of the woods perhaps. One poor fellow had almost reached his goal, and the others looked as though they were trying to follow his lead. Their heads were all pointing in the same direction. Gib and Billy stopped and stared at the dead soldiers for a long time, but for once, Billy was silent. Banjo whimpered and looked up at Billy as if to ask what this was all about.

General William Tecumseh Sherman (Library of Congress)

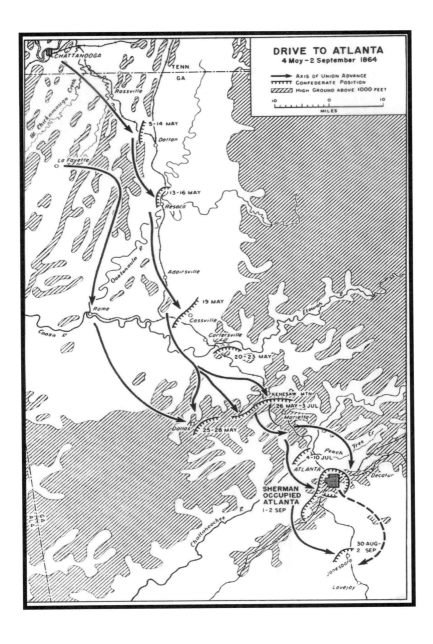

Chapter Nine

Battle of Peach Tree Creek

*You cannot qualify war in harsher terms than I will.
War is cruelty, and you cannot refine it.*
       Memoirs—**William T. Sherman**

"I request permission to visit my father, sir," Gib said to General Ward, one day shortly after the battle at Kennesaw Mountain. Now that Gib was an orderly at headquarters, he was no longer bunking with his father. The 79th Ohio was camped nearby, though, and for Gib it would be only a short ride when he wanted to visit his family and friends.

"Take a horse and keep your head down, son. There are snipers about," said General Ward. "Those Rebs will be looking to pick off any Yank, even a boy like you."

Gib saddled his horse and headed for the woods, thinking it best to keep off the road where he could become an easy target. The gray sky threatened rain, and the air was heavy with moisture. Gib rode slowly, enjoying the quiet of the forest after the hustle of headquarters. The Georgia forest was lush and green in early July. Even the air smelled green.

Gib saw a tree in front of him which seemed to have heavier foliage than the others. Even from a distance, he could see something moving high up in the tree. Could it be a hawk? As he approached the tree, Gib stopped and looked up through the branches. Above him was suspended the body of a Rebel soldier, hanging head downward. The dead soldier's eyes were open and they seemed to stare straight at Gib. Gib could see several bullet holes in the soldier's brown uniform where the blood had run out of him onto the ground below. The man hadn't been dead for very long Gib guessed, because the blood was still red and shiny against the cloth of the man's shirt. Gib's horse snickered and sidestepped, nervous at the smell of death. Gib shivered and urged the horse onward.

"I know who killed that Rebel," said Sergeant VanZandt when Gib told his father what he had seen in the forest. "That sharpshooter has been taking shots at our pickets all day. Wounded two of 'em. But we couldn't tell where he was."

"Why was he hanging in the tree?" Gib asked.

"Tied himself to a branch so's he could have full use of his hands for shooting at our boys, I s'pose," said Gib's father.

"How'd they spot him?" Gib asked.

"John Camp, the wagon master, said he could find him. Known for his hunting skills back in Wilmington, John is. John took a rifle and was able to locate the Reb when he took a shot. Turned out to be the last shot for Johnny Reb," said his father.

On his way back to headquarters, Gib took the road. If a minie ball was going to find him, he thought, it'd be easier to find his body on the road than in the woods.

The next day, the army was once again on the march to Atlanta. Their progress, which could once be measured by miles per day, was now measured in feet. The country was thickly wooded and the undergrowth dense. The rain-swollen creeks were difficult to cross. Gib and Billy were riding together on Betsy once again. There had been no horses to spare to replace Gib's Susie, though General Ward had promised Gib a pony just as soon as one could be found.

It was now July 5 and Sherman's army was looking for a way to cross the Chattahoochee River while General Kenner Garrard's cavalry occupied the mill town of Roswell. When Garrard found the town's mills producing cloth for Confederate uniforms, he wasted no time in getting the news to Sherman.

"We found the mills in full operation, sir," reported Garrard. "Rope. Canvas for tents. Butternut cloth. About 400 workers were employed."

"Burn the mills. Arrest the workers. March anyone connected to those mills under guard to Marietta and ship them by rail to the North as prisoners," replied Sherman.

"Bur sir, they are civilians and mostly women. What about their children?" asked Garrard.

"Let the women take along their children and clothing. But make no mistake, they are prisoners of war, male and female," Sherman replied.

Gib watched the citizens of Roswell load their wagons with clothing and food. Most were women and children, but there were a few men either too young or old to fight. Some were weeping and others had the vacant stares of the hopeless, resigned to their fate. Gib had seen that same expression on the faces of Confederate soldiers taken as prisoners many times. But Gib hadn't thought *civilians* could be made prisoners of war.

As the army got closer to Atlanta, Gib's corps was ordered to move double-quick time to a creek named Peachtree. On July 19th, the skirmishing with the Rebels was brisk and Gib was ordered to keep the regiment supplied with bullets and to gather the weapons of the men who were killed and wounded. Early in the day, Billy was sent away with a dispatch, and Gib watched him gallop away on his errand, wishing that he could go with him.

The next day, July 20, the fighting grew more intense. Gib was once again ordered to retrieve the guns and ammunition from the dead and wounded and carry them to the rear. All the while, he searched for his friend Billy. Was his friend dead? Had he been captured?

Early in the afternoon, Gib was summoned to headquarters.

"Boy, I need you to deliver this dispatch to the Colonel, said the officer. Near as I can tell the battle line is seven miles long.

Best way to reach the Colonel is through that corn field." Gib looked in the direction of the corn. In midsummer, the corn was plenty high enough to give him some cover in case he might be seen by a Confederate sniper.

"You can take that pony, and keep your head down," said the officer, but Gib was already mounting the small gray pony, with the dispatch securely buttoned inside his jacket. Just like Billy, he thought. Gib could be trusted with an important errand. Gib galloped the pony through the cornfield, bending low over the animal. He could hear the battle behind him and smell the acrid smoke of the gunpowder as he rode through the corn. He lifted his head and turned to look back at the battle, and suddenly, whommp!A minie ball slammed into the corn in front of him, and Gib knew that he had been spotted by a Confederate sharpshooter. He leaned low over the pony, urging her forward. Whomp, whomp, whomp! More minie balls whizzed by him and slammed into the corn. Kill me if you want to Johnny Reb, Gib thought as he raced on through the corn. He knew that his death was just one minie ball away, but he was not afraid. He might not deliver the dispatch that was tucked inside his blue shirt, but he would damned well die trying. Now he knew what Pap Doan meant when he said "duty is ours, the consequences are God's."

Gib sped through the corn with the bullets flying around him, and then finally he reached the edge of the field apparently out of the sharpshooter's range. He urged the tired pony, her sides heaving, into the shelter of some trees, and under cover of the woods he found his way to the colonel and delivered the dispatch as ordered.

Towards evening, Gib managed to catch of glimpse of Billy as Billy rode into view and reined his horse up beside Gib.

"Firing's pretty heavy west of the cornfields," said Billy with a grin. "Got hit right here, trying to get through the lines," said Billy and he thumped his chest with his fist.

"Shot!" said Gib, alarmed. His eyes searched Billy's uniform for signs of a wound, but he didn't see a drop of blood, just grime and road dust.

"Bullet would have gone straight through my heart but for the hardtack I keep in my breast pocket," said Billy. "Not even a minie ball can pierce those old worm castles. Why we ought to be loading our cannons with hardtack instead of cannonballs." Billy pulled the cracker from his pocket and sailed it through the air in the direction of the battle.

Gib smiled at his friend's joke. The hardtack cracker was now the biggest part of their diet. Tough and hard, and more often than not infested with worms, the men called them "teeth dullers." Gib and Billy always fried their hardtack in grease to soften them. How Gib longed for a loaf of soft, warm bread. Soon the war would be over, and he would get his fill.

"Guess we were both lucky not to get shot today," said Gib, thinking about his own close call in the cornfield. Suddenly, Gib heard a pop and he ducked as did the others who were standing in the clearing. When Gib looked up, he saw that Billy was falling forward on his horse. And then the horse reared up and the animal bolted as Billy's body slid to the ground. Gib shuddered as a cold wave of horror surged through him, and for a moment Gib wondered if he too had been shot. Others rushed to where he and Billy had been talking, and Gib could see that their mouths were moving, but he couldn't make out their words. And suddenly, Gib began to hear sounds so loud that he had to cover his ears to keep out the racket. A cow bawled in the pens and an uneasy horse whickered. A catbird complained loudly and a strong breeze rustled through the trees, and the sounds were so loud that Gib had to cover his ears. And then Gib heard another awful sound and realized that it was coming from himself. For the first time during this awful war, Gib began to cry. And then he felt his body lifted up by strong arms. Through his tears, Gib saw the kind face of General Newton, who carried him to the rear. Gib was too heartsick to be embarrassed, and he wrapped his arms around the big man's neck and sobbed unashamedly for his dear friend Billy.

Gib could barely choke out words. "We were going to see this war through together. I never thought any bullet could take the life out of one such as Billy Baner."

General Newton sat on a log and pulled the boy close to his chest. "A soldier's got to stop thinking in war time, Gib. Thinking is poison when you're ordered to shoot another man and knowing another man's been ordered to shoot you," said the General. Gib thought about Colonel Doan's words. Duty is ours but the consequences are God's. Now Billy had paid the ultimate price for doing his duty.

Later that evening when the battle had finally ended, Gib and Billy's mutt Banjo walked to the place where the dead had been carried. They found Billy's body in the shade of a tree with many others who had been killed on that day, among them, Gib's own cousin. He had been shot through the neck and had probably bled to death on the battlefield. Although he felt fresh sorrow at the sight of his cousin's body, Gib had no more tears left to cry. Banjo pawed and sniffed at Billy's body, and Gib thought his heart would break at the sight of it.

"He's gone, Banjo," Gib said to the animal and reached out to scratch his ears. The dog whimpered softly. Gib thought about all the boys who had died that day. Boys like Billy Baner and his cousin, who should have been playing with their dogs instead of having their youth cut short in war.

General Sherman (seated center) in council decides to raise the siege of Atlanta, sketched by Edwin Forbes. (Dover Pictorial Archives)

Chapter Ten

The Fall of Atlanta

There is many a boy here today who looks on war as all glory, but, boys, it is all hell. You can bear this warning voice to generations yet to come. I look upon war with horror. War is hell when you're getting licked.
Attributed to—W.T. Sherman

By the middle of August, after weeks of constant fighting and marching, General Sherman still had not succeeded in taking Atlanta. Then one day, Sherman's orders came to get ready to move. Gib's division was ordered to leave their camp at night, leaving the camp fires burning so the enemy would think the army was still there. At dawn they reached the Chattahoochee River, and it was while they were waiting there that Gib saw Sherman for the first time.

Sherman did not look like a great general to Gib. In fact he looked quite ordinary. Gib was surprised to see that the general wore shoes, not boots like the other officers. Why Gib's own father could have made those shoes, Gib thought. General Sherman and his staff rode up to them and dismounted, and the men shook hands all around. Then Sherman reached into his inside pocket and pulled out a cigar. He searched his pockets for a match, and finding none, looked around and then looked directly at Gib.

"Son, you are younger than I am. Won't you get me a light for my cigar?"

Gib ran as fast as he could to the cook's wagon to fetch a match. He returned to Sherman's side in less than five minutes and lit General Sherman's cigar.

"How old are you boy? Can't be much older than my son Willy," said the General, chewing on the end of his lit cigar. Gib knew that Sherman's 9-year-old son Willy had shown a keen military mind like his father and had become a favorite of the 13th U. S. Infantry. Sherman had been inconsolable when the boy had died of typhoid.

"Older than I look, sir," replied Gib. He didn't want the General to think he wasn't old enough for soldiering. Sherman smiled, but then turned back to his staff.

"Quickest way to end this war with the least bloodshed is to destroy property. We'll make the South sick of it all, without any unnecessary killing," said Sherman. "When we take Atlanta, women and children and peaceful non combatants are not to be injured. Those are my orders."

Finally, on September 2, 1864, the Union army seized Atlanta. The troops, including Gib, settled down in the battered city. All of the citizens of Atlanta were ordered to get out. Gib watched the residents leave their fine houses, carrying what belongings they could pack into carts, wagons and buggies. As soon as a house was vacated, soldiers went in, ripping off floor boards, shutters, anything to fix up their own quarters in the camps. Other houses were completely dismantled and the lumber was carted away to build temporary quarters for the officers.

On Nov. 15, the army left Atlanta. But before they left, they leveled Atlanta's railroad depot and set fire to the buildings. The flames quickly spread to other buildings, including an oil refinery, theaters, the jail, and the Atlanta Hotel, and soon the whole city was ablaze, the smoke rising high in the air and hanging over the ruined city. All that remained were 400 houses and a few churches. And then they left the ruins of Atlanta behind and headed east. Where were they going? Nobody knew. Nearly 25,000 freed slaves followed along both sides of the army, enjoying their first taste of freedom.

The army marched ten miles a day, a leisurely pace even for Gib. The heart of enemy country was rich with farms that were well supplied with food for the troops. Gib spent much of his time foraging on the countryside and liking it. Chickens, turkeys and cattle were seized for slaughter. Loaves of bread, crocks of jam and preserves and chunks of ham were carried back to camp. Gib had not eaten better since he had left Port William.

Sherman's men tearing up the railroad tracks in Atlanta, photographed by George N. Barnard (Library of Congress)

The army was ordered not to destroy property or take things they didn't need for the march, but Gib knew that some of the men were looting the abandoned homes along the route. Other soldiers were ordered to protect the homes and belongings of the army as they marched through Georgia. Once, Gib's own father had been ordered to guard a house filled with women and children and when they left, the lady of the house had presented Gib's father with a fine purse to thank him for helping. Another time, some of the men had been fired on by Rebel soldiers hiding in one of the houses along the route, and when the Union soldiers drove them off they discovered that the Rebels had looted the house and taken everything. It seemed to Gib that the war had brought out the best, and the worst, in just about everybody on all sides, soldiers as well as civilians.

Impressed by Lil Gib's bravery at the battle of Peachtree Creek, his friends in the 79th Ohio agreed that Gib needed a pony. One day while they were camped outside Milledgeville, the capital of Georgia, Lieutenant Harryman presented Gib with a pony confiscated from a Confederate farm.

"Just the right size for you, lad," said Lieutenant Harryman, "tho' she looks more like a lady than a war pony. Don't imagine she's been battle tested."

"Don't have to be big to be brave," said Gib. "She'll measure up."

Finally! A pony of his own! Gib took the reins and looked into the animal's eyes—not up into the eyes, but straight into the eyes of the loveliest little pony he had ever seen. He smoothed her glossy mane with his palm and buried his face into her warm, soft neck and breathed in the goodness of the horse flesh. Someone must have loved this pony very much, he thought, to keep her so plump and well groomed. He wondered if perhaps some Confederate child had owned this pony and must right now be grieving her loss. Gib felt bad about that.

"What shall I call her?" Gib asked. Many of the confiscated Confederate horses were named "Reb" but Gib didn't think that name fit this gorgeous little animal.

"That's for you to say, lad," said Lieutenant Harryman, and he reined his own horse away.

For the next few days while the army was camped in Milledgeville, Gib spent every spare moment with his pony. She was short enough so that he could climb upon her back easily and Gib enjoyed prancing her though the camp to show her off. But he couldn't think of a name worthy enough for so fine a pony.

Lexington was Sherman's favorite horse, but he also rode Dolly and Sam. Mother Bickerdyke rode Old Whitey, and Major General Hooker rode Lookout. Major General Logan rode Slasher and Major General McClellan named his favorite mounts Kentuck and Daniel Webster. Gib couldn't think of a good enough name for his pony.

One day when the army was marching through town, Gib on his new pony, he passed a house where three pretty young girls were standing in front. Two of the girls scowled at him, and one of the girls whirled around and stomped off up the steps and into the house as the invaders rode by. But the youngest, a girl who looked to be about Gib's age, just stood there watching as they approached. When their eyes met, Gib reined his pony over her way.

"Yankee," the older girl spat out at him, and Gib had not known such hatred could be directed towards him until now. "Go home, Yankee. You've destroyed everything, and still you want more!" she said, and she too stomped off into the house.

"Are you going to burn our house?" asked the girl, looking up at Gib on his pony. She reminded him a bit of Masie Furnace, with her green eyes and braided hair.

"Don't imagine so," said Gib, though Sherman's men had destroyed hundreds of buildings in recent weeks. This time, however, the men were on the move, and Gib didn't think they'd be ordered to stop and burn houses.

The pony lowered her head and nudged the little girl.

"What's her name?" asked the girl, reaching out to scratch the pony's ears.

"Haven't yet named her," Gib admitted.

"You can use my name if you like," said the girl. "My name is Fannie Lee."

Fannie Lee. It was a good name for a pony too, Gib thought. And the army had taken so much from these people the least he could do was name his pony for the girl.

There was a sharp command of "Forward march!" and Gib, riding Fannie Lee, fell in with the other soldiers as they marched through the town.

Freed Slaves welcoming the Union Army, sketched by Edwin Forbes. (Dover Pictorial Archives)

Chapter Eleven

Incident at Ebenezer Creek

When the men reached a rail line, they took up the rails and heated them so they could bend them around trees into fancy shapes they called "Sherman's neckties." Another favorite shape to make was the letters U. S.

"The Rebs could just put the rails back if we didn't bend 'em," Gib's friend Lieutenant Harryman explained. Lieutenant Harryman had taken Gib under his wing after Billy's death and Gib was grateful for the comfort of it. Lieutenant Harryman had also taken in Banjo.

"Destroying the rail lines cuts off supplies to the enemy so's to bring this war to a close." It all made sense to Gib. Anything to get this war done with, he thought as he rode behind the older man. Gib and Lieutenant Harryman often rode together on foraging expeditions.

The army made good use of *The Battle Hymn of the Republic* and *John Brown's Body* as they marched south and east, apparently toward the sea. On each side of the marching army, Gib could see thousands of freed slaves, dancing, singing, and praying. As Sherman rode through the hordes of freed slaves, they reached out to touch his stirrups and pressed their heads into the sides of his horse, Sam.

"He's the Angel of the Lord!" one old black woman had cried out. Men, women and children hugged the soldiers, crying and sighing and singing.

Sometimes the black men helped to make the sandy roads passable for the wagons, and the army fed them or paid them in return for their labor, but as they got closer to the sea, they found fewer farms and fewer supplies.

"General Davis says the Negroes are slowing down the march. He and General Sherman are eager to reach Savannah by Christmas," said Lieutenant Harryman to Gib one day in early December.

"You mean General Reb?" he asked. Gib remembered the hot-headed Davis, who had killed General Nelson when they were camped in Louisville. He never served a day in prison for what some thought was outright murder of a fellow officer. His men called him General Reb because he shared the same name as the Confederate President, Jefferson Davis.

"His men don't much like him and he don't much like them. Fightin' and cussin' are his specialty, they say," said Lieutenant Harryman.

A few days later, Gib and the others got the news that General Davis had found a way to solve his problem with the freed slaves. Gib's father brought the news to Gib.

"The men of the XIV Corps laid a pontoon bridge across a stream called Ebenezer Creek. After the army crossed it, General Davis ordered his men to cut the ropes and pull the bridge up on the bank, leaving the fugitive followers behind them," said Sergeant VanZandt. Gib could hardly believe his own army could be so cruel.

"Didn't they try to swim across?" Gib asked.

"Some did, but the creek was swollen and many were swept downstream and drowned. Others tried to cross on rafts, but they sank. Pretty soon some Confederate raiders came out of the woods and those who were still on the bank were shot and slashed to death."

"Didn't anyone try to help them?" said Gib.

"The orders given were to take up the pontoon and not let a Negro cross; seems the orders were followed to the letter."

It seemed also to Gib that emancipation for these Negroes had been brief indeed.

The Union troops stormed Fort McCallister late in the afternoon of December 13. The assault lasted only 15 minutes. On Christmas Eve, Sherman sent a telegram to President Lincoln that said, "I beg to present you as a Christmas gift the city of Savannah." Surely the war must soon come to an end now, Gib thought.

In Savannah, Gib, riding Fannie Lee, saw the sea for the first time. He also had his first taste of oysters, which he thought the most delicious thing he had eaten since he'd joined the army. Oyster stew, oysters on the half shell, roast oysters, fried oysters—Gib couldn't eat enough of them. Sherman had given his army orders to rest while they were in Savannah. Gib and Fannie Lee rode through the streets of the stately old city during the warm afternoons. He drew pay, along with the other men, for the first time in months, but found that prices for luxuries were high. Apples, which were Fannie Lee's favorite treat, sold for $50 a barrel. A haircut, which Gib sorely needed, cost 75 cents.

While they were camped in the city, Sherman organized classes for the men in military education to keep his troops busy during the day. There were drills, formations, and dress parades. But at night, Gib and the others attended concerts and theatricals.

Soon, Sherman's men prepared to leave Georgia and enter South Carolina, the first state to secede, and according to Sherman, the state that bore the major blame for the war.

The army issued changes of uniform and new blankets, but many of the men, refused them.

"Long march ahead once we leave Savannah. Don't need no excess baggage," said Lieutenant Harryman. Banjo sat beside them and thumped his tail on the ground.

"Guess I'll be taking the shoes at least," Gib replied. Although he hadn't grown an inch in the three years he'd been with the army, his feet had finally outgrown the shoes his father had made for him.

As the army marched north, the rain was unceasing. Gib rode Fannie Lee part of the way, but took pity on the pony as she struggled over the boggy roads. Even though it was hard to keep up with the other men, Gib preferred to walk beside Fannie Lee rather than put more of a burden on her. The rain kept coming. Even in camp, which they made on the highest ground, the men and horses sometimes waded in six inches of water. But by the middle of February, Sherman's soldiers had reached Columbia, the capital of South Carolina. On February 17, Gib and Fannie Lee watched from a hillside as the army began to shell the city. He saw plumes of smoke already rising from the railroad depot. Gib saw three men ride toward the army, one of them carrying a white flag. The Confederate army had surrendered the capital city without so much as a fight!

Gib rode Fannie Lee across the pontoon bridge into the city, moving through the roaring throngs of civilians. Some were Northern sympathizers who welcomed them, but most were Southerners who hated them. Even those who welcomed them had fear in their eyes, for Sherman's army struck terror in their hearts. They remembered Atlanta.

"We'll destroy no private property," Sherman had declared once inside the surrendered city of Columbia. But by nightfall, a riot had broken out in the streets and fires raged uncontrolled throughout the city. Most of Columbia burned to the ground.

The morning after the fire, Gib and Fannie Lee rode through the blackened debris and smoldering embers. The trees that once shaded the streets of the beautiful city stood out against the sky like skeletons. All that was left of the stately mansions were lone chimneys rising out of the smoking rubble. Some citizens sat atop piles of belongings they had been able to save from the fire, weeping or with stunned looks upon their faces. One woman sat with her children upon a mattress, with fine paintings and sculpture strewn around them. The children were crying. Gib saw one man sitting near a pile of broken furniture with his head bowed into his hands. Without homes, without property, Gib wondered what would become of these people.

The army moved northward from Columbia, with little Confederate resistance, toward N. Carolina. Sherman had vowed to bring the entire South to its knees and end the war once and for all.

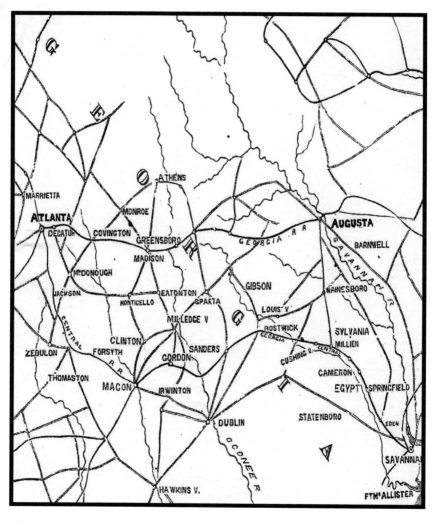

Map showing the march from Atlanta to Savannah and the sea.

Chapter Twelve

"He knew no fear"

This noble little trusty and brave soldier took the order; and in less than thirty minutes returned. Through the thickest of shot and shell, he displayed the noblest bravery, and other members of the staff will cite you noble deeds of bravery done by him. Though but a child soldier, he knew no fear.
  Letter to General, R. A. Alger, Secretary of War from
  William Hardenbrook, Lieut. and Cap. Co. H,
  70th Ind. Vol. Inf., 1898, Bentonville, NC

It was the first all-out fighting that Gib had seen since the long, bloody struggle for Atlanta. Gib watched as the long line of Rebels swept across the fields as far as the eye could see. The gray line had driven back the Union troops for miles. Gib had never seen such fighting. Gib had taken Fannie Lee to the rear for safety, but then returned to General Ward's side in case he was called to carry a dispatch.

"My God! The men need to rest. The guns are too hot," said the General as they watched the spectacle of the battle from the hillside. But the firing continued into the afternoon and it seemed that the two lines, one blue and one gray, were going to fight it out. When the blue line looked like it was giving way, General Ward summoned Gib.

"Take this dispatch to Captain Gery. We need all available men and artillery to support those men. Make haste, young man, or the day will be lost!" said the General. "You'll have to take your pony. My horse has been wounded."

Gib tucked the message inside his coat and sprinted to the rear where he had tied Fannie Lee. He leapt upon her back and raced off towards the left flank of the fighting where he knew Captain Gery's men probably had a fight of their own. Minie balls whizzed around Gib and Fannie Lee. The sounds of the minie balls differed, depending on how close they came to something solid. "Rat a tat tat," went the minie balls that slammed into the earth around him as Gib and Fannie Lee rushed headlong through the clearing. Another minie sounded like a kitten's cry as it sped by his ear, knocking off his hat. Gib feared for Fannie Lee. A boy on a pony was sure to be a dispatcher, and shooting the pony would pretty much ensure that an important message never got delivered. Gib bent low over Fannie Lee, her sides heaving with exertion, but the pony never hesitated, even when a minie ball grazed her flank. Gib saw blood ooze from the wound. Gib remembered the time that Susie had been shot out from under him. Not Fannie Lee! But the pony raced forward. Then suddenly, the battle sounds were in the distance and Gib could hear different sounds now, not battle sounds. Somewhere, a dog barked. A crow cawed high overhead, and a rooster crowed on an unseen farm.

And then Captain Gery and his men were in sight. Quickly, Gib delivered the message. He was relieved to see that Fannie Lee's injury was a flesh wound, but there was not time to tend to it then. Captain Gery was gathering his men and artillery.

"You'll have to take us back to the fighting. Show us the quickest way to the front," shouted Captain Gery.

Gib and Fannie Lee led the way. The exhausted pony never faltered, even as they approached the din of battle. As they got closer to the front, Gib's senses heightened--especially his hearing. Above the din of the gunfire he could now hear other sounds. He heard the excited cries of the soldiers as they struggled in battle, and he heard the pitiful moans of the wounded as they fell and cried out for help. Horses screamed in terror. Others screamed in pain as they were shot out from under their riders. Gib could tell the difference in the sounds the horses made, whether a horse was just terrified of the battle or if it had been shot. But Fannie Lee galloped forward towards these terrifying sounds, carrying Gib and leading the reinforcements.

It was now April. Gib and the rest of the XX Corps were on the march to Raleigh, when they spotted a staff officer galloping up the road towards them, shouting and waving his arms. At first Gib thought that the officer was warning them. Sensing danger, Gib's hearing sharpened so that he heard before the others just what the officer was yelling.

"Lee's surrendered!" the officer shouted as he drew nearer.

As the officer rode through the throng of men, the soldiers began throwing their hats up into the air, and they all began cheering. Gib flung his own kepi high into the air. And then all hell broke loose. Cracker boxes, blankets and knapsacks rained from the sky and men cheered themselves hoarse. One man leaped into the air, cracked his heels together and turned a somersault right in the road.

The celebration continued into the evening as the men passed around cups of strong drink About midnight, the regimental band began to play what sounded like *John Brown's Body*, but by the time they got to the end, the musicians seemed to be playing two or three different tunes all at once. Gib made his way to the place where he had tied up Fannie Lee to keep her out of harm's way when the entire ruckus began. The pony's wound was healing nicely, Gib noted. He put his arms around Fannie Lee's neck and hugged her, but the animal pulled away looking for the customary treat. Gib pulled a hard tack cracker from his pocket and offered it to her. Fannie Lee sniffed at it delicately, but refused it.

"Sorry, baby girl," said Gib. "Next time, I'll bring you an apple. And soon this war will be over and we'll go home and you'll have all the apples that you care to eat!"

Chapter Thirteen

On to Washington

After the surrender, Gib and Fannie Lee marched north with the army, passing through Richmond, the capital of the Confederacy. Here Gib and Lieutenant Harryman toured Libby Prison, where Gib's uncle had been taken prisoner. The three-story brick warehouse had been used only for Union officers.

"Did they release the prisoners before the surrender?" Gib asked. Perhaps his uncle was already home in Port William.

"Had to clear out this prison long before. Too much overcrowding! Confederates sent the prisoners from here down to Macon last year," he answered.

The army rested at Richmond for a few days. Curious, Gib and Lieutenant Harryman stood before Robert E. Lee's tall brick house on Franklin Street, hoping for a glimpse of the famous General who had just returned from the surrender site of Appomattox. They wandered around the burned and charred sections of the once beautiful city, and then climbed around on the earthworks that had been put up to keep them out.

"Don't hold a candle to the earthworks we faced at Atlanta, do they Gib?" asked Lieutenant Harryman.

"Naw, we coulda walked right over these," Gib agreed, but to Gib the ruins of Atlanta seemed a long time ago.

Then, the troops continued their march north to Washington. They stopped at Fredericksburg so the men could see the famous battlefield. The landscape was still torn from the cannon fire. Tree trunks were pocked with musket balls, and in places Gib could see the whitened skeletons of Union soldiers.

At Chancellorsville, Gib found a tree still red with the blood of the wounded—and more bones. Finally, the army reached Mount Vernon, where they marched slowly around Washington's mansion and saluted as they passed his tomb. They settled into makeshift camps on the filthy, littered army fields on the outskirts of the nation's capital. Now that the soldiering was done with, Gib settled in again with the men of Port William and the 79th Ohio. The 79th had gone into the field with 900 men but would return with fewer than half that number.

In Washington Gib gave himself up to a bit of touring. Here were great government buildings. With his father and uncles, Gib toured the Capitol's picture gallery and climbed the steps to the dome. He visited the Navy Yard with its powerful warships. With his former teacher Mr. Bodkin and his cousin, Gib strolled the streets from one end of the city to the other, and as he walked by one storefront, Gib stopped to stare at his reflection in the windowpane. He barely recognized himself. His face had lost much of its boyishness, and lines creased his forehead. It took him a moment to realize that the reflection in the glass was that of a man. Why Masie Furnace wouldn't even recognize him, Gib thought. He was ready to go home. There was just one more order to obey before the troops were mustered out.

"Going to be a big parade through the streets of Washington next month," said Lieutenant Harryman. "Both Union armies are going to march—it'll take two days. The Easterners of the army of the Potomac will march one day and those of us in Sherman's army will march the second day."

Gib was glad that Sherman's men would march the second day. Uncle Billy's men would outshine the troops of the army of the Potomac. Sure, the Easterners had seen some hard fighting, but nothing on the scale of Sherman's Western army!

"Fannie Lee's carried me more'n a thousand miles. I guess she'll be happy to carry me a few more before we get shipped back to Port William," said Gib.

Lieutenant Harryman looked hard at Gib. "You won't be taking that pony to Ohio. It doesn't belong to you."

Gib was stunned. He'd have to give up Fannie Lee? Why?

"Union horses or those taken as contraband, like Fannie Lee, belong to the U.S. government."

"Doesn't seem right that the Rebs can keep their horses but I have to give up Fannie Lee," Gib said.

"Southerners need their horses to help plow for spring planting," Lieutenant Harryman explained.

"Well I need Fannie Lee. And she needs me."

But, before Gib could take it all in, other news reached the camp. It quickly sent the camp into a tailspin.

"President Lincoln has been murdered! Shot through the head in his private box at Ford's Theatre. Andrew Johnson has already been sworn in as President," shouted the messenger.

The north side of Libby Prison in Richmond, VA, photographed after the war. (Library of Congress)

Chapter Fourteen

An Interview with the President

June 1865
Farewell Message from Sherman to his Troops:

The time has come for us to part. Our work is done, and armed enemies no longer defy us. Some of you will go to your homes, and others will be retained in military service.

How far the operations of this army contributed to the final overthrow of the Confederacy must be judged by others, not by us; but you have done all that men could do, and we have a right to join in the universal joy that fills our land because the war is over.

Your general now bids you farewell, with the full belief that, as in war, you have been good soldiers; so, in peace, you will make good citizens; and if, unfortunately, new wars should arise in your country, "Sherman's army" will be first to buckle on its old armor and come forth to defend and maintain the government of our inheritance.

Gib washed his tattered clothes in the river to prepare for the parade. He polished his sword and the brass trim on his drum. Then he curried Fannie Lee and cleaned her hooves. The parade might be the last chance Gib had to ride Fannie Lee, and he wanted them both to look their best.

Yesterday, the Easterners of the Army of the Potomac had marched for six hours through the streets of Washington in their newly issued uniforms, their officers complete with white gloves. But Sherman had directed his "bummers" to wear their clean and mended battle weary clothes when it was their turn to march. Some might wear new hats or pants, but many others would march barefoot for lack of shoes. Sherman's "bummers" would be a sharp contrast to the army of the Potomac's dandified display, thought Gib.

Today, May 24, Gib would ride Fannie Lee down Pennsylvania Avenue proudly with the staff of the Third Division, Twentieth Corps. At five a.m. the sergeants began barking the roll call, and the column moved into position to begin the parade. At 9 a.m. the signal gun fired for the procession to begin. Gib, mounted on Fannie Lee at the head of the column, his little sword strapped to his side and his drum fastened to the pony's saddle, went forward to meet the cheering crowd. Inside the drum was the coin Lieutenant Ellwood had given Gib for drumming up the recruits. This he would keep as a reminder of what he had gained when he joined the army. Inside the drum was Anna's gift, the buckeye that Gib had carried through the war to remind him of all that he had left behind in Port William when he enlisted. And then there was the pair of tiny shoes he had found on the battlefield. These shoes he would keep to remind him of those who would never be able to return home now that the war was finally over. Gib knew that some of the soldiers would bring the war home with them, even though the real fighting was done. Those soldiers would be fighting for the rest of their lives. Others, like Gib, himself, would put the war and fighting behind them. All he would bring home from the war was a tiny pair of shoes.

Gib kept his back straight and his eyes forward as the column moved forward. Crowds of spectators lined the street. Banners hung overhead:
THE PUBLIC SCHOOLS OF WASHINGTON
WELCOME THE HEROES OF THE REPUBLIC.
HONOR TO THE BRAVE!

Another banner proclaimed:
HAIL TO THE WESTERN HEROES!
Sometimes the spectators threw flowers at the marching troops, but Sherman's bummers kept marching, eyes straight ahead as they had been ordered to do. Gib heard the roaring of the troops far ahead of his regiment and soon saw the cause of it. An American flag flew from a pole at the road side and beneath it was an old man with a long beard and flowing hair who bowed at the soldiers as they marched by.

The Grand Review: units of the 20th Army Corps passing on Pennsylvania Avenue, Washington D.C., photographed by Matthew Brady. (Library of Congress)

Looking up Pennsylvania Avenue from the Treasury Building during the passage of Sherman's grand army. (Library of Congress)

This record filled out by VanZandt in 1915 shows the Civil War veteran's birthdate to be Dec. 20, 1851, making him age 10 at the time of his enlistment. (Courtesy Dennis Keesee)

"When they fired on Fort Sumter, I vowed I'd never shave nor cut my hair til this flag waved o'er the whole country once again," the man shouted.

The regimental drums beat out the march. General Augur, commander of the District of Columbia had offered his two magnificent bands for Sherman's parade through the city, but Sherman had said he preferred his own campaign-weary regimental bands. The musicians played and the drummers beat out a rhythm for the men. Rat a tat tat, down Pennsylvania Avenue went the army to the cheering, enthusiastic spectators. Someone in the crowd stepped forward and put a wreath of flowers around Fannie Lee's neck, but Gib kept his eyes straight forward as he urged the pony onward, a part of the moving line of bright blue glittering with steel of polished guns.

Someone in the crowd called out "What regiment?" A soldier behind Gib cried out "79th Ohio!" And the crowd broke out in cheers. Somewhere behind him, Mother Bickerdyke rode on her horse, Old Whitey, wearing her sunbonnet and calico dress. The crowd cheered her as a symbol of the Union's triumph. And somewhere behind him, Gib knew that Banjo trotted along beside the regiment he had adopted after the death of his master Billy Baner.

In contrast to the cheering and pageantry on the street, the porches and balconies were draped in black in mourning for the assassinated President. As Gib neared the Treasury Building, he was surprised to see General Sherman wearing what looked to be a new uniform, mounted on Lexington. As General Sherman neared the reviewing stand where the government officials sat, he waved and approached the men. President Johnson, General Grant, and Secretary of War Stanton were there and rose to greet Sherman, who shook hands with the President and then General Grant, but Gib thought that the General ignored Stanton's outstretched hand. It was rumored that the Secretary of War had no love for their Uncle Billy. Then General Sherman turned to review his troops.

Two days after the parade, Lieutenant Harryman visited Gib in camp. The officer found Gib sitting with his father outside the tent that they shared. The men of the 79th were waiting their turn to be shipped home to Ohio by train. The parade had marked the official end of their obligation to the army. When Gib had first joined the army, he had been all about the adventure and the glory and the duty to preserve the Union. Then he had embraced the cause of abolition and freeing the slaves. Now that it was all accomplished, Gib just wanted to go home.

"President Johnson summons you, Gib! He says he wants to meet the little fellow who marched with General Sherman to the sea," said Lieutenant Harryman.

That afternoon, Gib and Lieutenant Harryman went to call upon the President. President Johnson was sitting at a large mahogany table, scattered with papers. He looked up when Gib and Lieutenant Harryman were led into the room.

"And how is it that so small a boy should come to be with the army?" President Johnson asked. Although the President was looking at Gib, he seemed to be addressing Lieutenant Harryman.

"Sir, this young man joined up as a drummer with his Pa early in the war. He was made an orderly and came bravely through many a heated battle with the rest of his division," Lieutenant Harryman told the President about Gib's actions at Resaca and Bentonville.

The President stood up and took off his spectacles, and he leaned over the cluttered table regarding Gib.

"Draw regular army pay, then, young man?"

"Yes sir!" replied Gib.

"Seeing as how you served your country so bravely, there might be something more I can do for you. Now then…," the President began. Gib didn't wait for the man to finish his thought before he blurted out:

"Sir, I should like to keep the pony that took me through the worst of it. I should like to take her home with me to Ohio."

"Your pony? Union horses are government property. I think you'd want a commission in the army now that the fighting's over once and for all. Why a commission in the army would set you up for life. Which is it boy, the pony or the commission in the army?" asked the President.

For the most part, Gib's soldiering would remain the most important, grand experience of his life. And if there was anything good with that experience, and there was, it was that Gib had an unshaken faith in his fellow human beings. No one who'd witnessed the fighting at Kennesaw Mountain or Resaca or Peachtree Creek or Bentonville would ever doubt the courage and resolve of their fellow human beings. But did Gib want to be a soldier now? No way. Gib was done with soldiering.

"Sir, I choose Fannie Lee. She's the one who brought me through the end of this war business, and now that it's over, I feel I owe her," said Gib.

"Most boys your age would have chosen the commission," said President Johnson, slowly sitting down. He drew a blank sheet of paper from the file and began to write.

"With all respect, sir, war sometimes makes us into people we didn't know we were," Gib replied.

At least that was true for Gib. He had seen more than the elephant, and he had not been found wanting. Much of what he had seen and done would be etched finer in his memory than in fact. Gib wondered what historians would say about the events he'd witnessed. He had been battle tested, but he wanted no more of it. Gib wanted to return with Fannie Lee to Port William and once there, he would continue his schooling and maybe become a teacher like Mr. Bodkin.

Or perhaps he would learn to make shoes.

President Andrew Johnson (Library of Congress)

Author's Note and Acknowledgments

I am indebted to The Research Council of Kent State University for the support which made possible the research and writing of this book. I first learned about Gilbert VanZandt (sometimes spelled Vanzant) and his wartime bravery from a marker erected by the Ohio Bicentennial Commission to celebrate the state's 200th birthday. The marker, dedicated Nov. 7, 1999, recognizes Gilbert VanZandt as an American hero, but it tells only part of the story. It wasn't until I contacted Wilmington, Ohio realtor and Civil War researcher, Gary Kersey, that I learned about Fannie Lee. I am indebted to Gary who spent a day with me in the fall of 2002, showing me the Clinton County area and sharing with me his own considerable research about the hero of this story.

Many other people helped me to piece this story together. Thanks to Sally Van Sant Sondesky, Historian of the VanZandt Society, for sharing information in the organization's files. Thanks also to Kay Fisher, Director of the Clinton County (Ohio) Historical Society and to Jeff Bridgers, Reference Librarian, Library of Congress, for leads on photographs and other information. I am grateful to Dennis Keesee, author of *Too Young to Die, Boy Soldiers of the Union Army 1861-1865,* who generously shared his file of research on Lil Gib, including Gib's military records. Thanks again to Dr. Tom Davis, professor emeritus at Kent State University, for reading drafts. And of course, I thank my husband Roland for his support and encouragement during the writing of this book.

Gilbert VanZandt was different in many ways from his fellow soldiers. Here is some of what we know about the soldier called Lil Gib:

He was one of the youngest boys in what has been called "The Boys' War." Gilbert VanZandt was born in Port William, Clinton County, Ohio on Dec. 20, 1851. When he enlisted in the Union army on August 6, 1862, he was ten years, seven months and 16 days old, making him one of the youngest, if not the youngest boy to enlist on either side. Another Ohio boy, 8-year-old drummer boy Avery Brown, has also been commemorated as the Civil War's youngest enlisted soldier. However, a number of claimants on each side—Confederate and Union—vie for the honor of having been the youngest enlistee.

According to the *Photographic History of the Civil War*, at least 25 boys were ten or under at time of Federal enlistment, and 300 were 13 or under. One regiment, the 43rd Ohio, was known as the "boy regiment," because of its youthfulness. Of the 330 teenagers in that regiment, 39 lost their lives during military service. Most of the boys in the Civil War were fifers or drummers, but they were regularly enrolled and sometimes they were fighters. Gilbert VanZandt himself never made claim to being the youngest, but some who wrote about Lil Gib staked such a claim on his behalf.

We also know that Lil Gib was small in stature, even for his age. In a letter written to recommend Lil Gib for a medal of honor, one officer wrote: "He was so small that he could not mount his horse; so, we had to find him a pony. VanZandt, only twelve years old and small for his age, did full duty all through." Reportedly, Gib's discharge papers stated that Lil Gib stood only four feet tall, no inches, at the end of the war when he was 13. The average height of a solider during the Civil War was between five feet five inches and five feet nine.

Gib's parents surely must have tried to dissuade their son from joining the army, but reportedly Gib was determined. His mother, however, thought that Gib was only going off to help recruit soldiers, and she even made him a uniform for that activity. When Gib marched out of town in July of 1862, she probably thought he would return to her once the recruiting and training duties were done. But Gib was to be gone for three years. She is quoted as saying, "War times make folks do funny things, and they stole him from me, really, his father and the rest, and took him down to Fort Dennison, and then, first thing I knew he was enlisted." Gib was able to stay in close contact with his father, uncle and cousins throughout much of the war.

Although it seems incredible today that any youth, especially one so small in stature, could have withstood the atrocities and hardships of the Civil War for three years, it was not Gib's youth and size that impressed me so much as his actions. He rose above his youth and his size to fulfill his obligations. And when it was all over, Lil Gib did a big thing for such a little boy—he decided to leave the military life behind for good.

After the war, Gilbert "Lil Gib" VanZandt returned to Port William, where he resumed his schooling for three more years. Fannie Lee was shipped by train to nearby Wilmington, Ohio, where she eventually became a great favorite of Gib's younger brother Johnnie, born in 1869. Fannie Lee must have lived to be quite an old pony for some people remembered Johnnie galloping her up and down the streets of Xenia, Ohio, where the family had moved after the war.

During his lifetime, Gib worked at a variety of occupations, including teacher, farmer, clerk, salesman, store manager and cowboy. He must have been restless, because he moved frequently, establishing homes in Ohio, Illinois, Wyoming, Washington D.C., Kansas and Missouri. Gib never married. He died in Kansas City, Missouri in 1944 at age 92. Reportedly, he never talked much about his war experiences, but his official discharge had a place of honor in his home during his final years in Kansas City. It read:

To all whom it may concern:
Know ye that Gilbert VanZandt, Drummer, of Captain Edward L. Patterson's Company D, 79th Regiment, Ohio Infantry Volunteers, who was enrolled on the 31st day of October, One

Thousand Eight Hundred and Sixty-two, to serve for three years or during the war, is hereby discharged from the service of the United States, this 9th day of June, One Thousand Eight Hundred and Sixty-five, near Washington, D. C. by order of the Secretary of War. (No objection to his being re-enlisted is known to exist.)

Said Gilbert VanZandt was born in Clinton County, Ohio; is 13 years of age; 4 feet no inches high; light complexion; blue eyes; light hair; and by occupation when enrolled, a Drummer.

Given near Washington D. C. this 9th day of June, 1865.

(signed) *A. W. Sloan*
Lieut. Colonel, Commanding Regiment.

An article by J. F. Orr in *The* (Xenia) *Gazette* may have inspired this poem about Lil' Gib and Fannie Lee.

Little Gib

By. W. C. Tichenor (1938)

*"Little Gib, of the Seventy-Ninth
Ohio volunteers
Was a drummer boy but ten years old
But brave despite his years.*

*When a lieutenant came with a six-mule team
Recruiting soldiers to serve
Little Gib volunteered to drum for him
And drum he did with nerve.*

*Lieutenant Elwood so pleased was he
He gave Gib fifty cents.
That was the first coin that Gib had earned
And his pleasure was intense.*

*Then out thru the country with Captain Hicks
To drum up recruits went he,
Imagining war was a gala thing
And battle a pleasantry.*

*His school teacher, father and twenty young friends
Enlisted to serve the flag;
All were models of manhood; behind them
"Gib," determined not to lag.*

And how the boys of the country-side
Did envy "Little Gib"!
With his drumsticks beating time to march
And his belt across his rib!

For nearly three months he marched along
Fearing he might be rejected;
But glad was he when the word came on:
"Little Gib has been selected."

His mother never meant him to go,
Tho he helped to "get, the men;
But he enlisted and off he went;
What could his mother do then?

And away he marched with Company D,
"Drumming to beat the band";
And many a heart beat fast at sight
Of the drummer boy in the land.

At Dennison he met with Mister Gray Back,
The pest of soldiers in the war;
At Louisville he heard how Davis
Killed Nelson without a scar.

At Nashville they fitted "Gib, out anew
With little sword and drum,
And his messmates often stood at salute
When they saw their favorite come.

When Little Gib was mustered in
His father he often saw;
But after the fight at Resaca's field
He missed him till Kennesaw.

But good "Pap, Doan was colonel now,
And loved him as his own.
He treated Gib with more regard
Than if he were full-grown.

The only time Little Gib felt grief,
Or shed a boyish tear
Was when his pal Billy Baner was shot
And carried to the rear.

He never murmured at war's hardships,
Bore storm and heat and cold,
And passed thru all with a courage rate
With soldiers thirty years old.

And only once was he in fault
For failure to beat the "Call";
And he served a day for negligence
Of duty, and that was all.

He saw a Rebel soldier hanging
Head down from a leafy tree;
A wagon-master had shot him—
Sharp-shooter no more was he.

A group of prisoner boys were crying—
Had been told they'd lose their ears.
Little Gib told them "You needn't worry,"
And they brushed away their tears.

He never felt homesick but once—
When back from a short furlough—
He thought of his mother and his friends
Beyond the Ohio.

"Most gentlemanly little fellow"

*Reported Captain Snell.
"Modest in his demeanor, too,
As all his comrades tell."*

*With the band he continued playing the drum
Till marches grew too hard,
When he was detailed as a messenger
At headquarters of General Ward.*

*Too small to mount a horse was Gib,
A pony he must have;
And when they got to Milledgeville
A pony the soldiers gave.*

*The pony commandeered for him
He named her Fannie Lee
In honor of a Southern girl—
A touch of chivalry.*

*And often midst the battle's din
Little Gib went galloping by
On Fannie Lee, his trusty mount,
A full-fledged orderly.*

*Four feet and ten years of patriotism
Were in that little man
As he beat the drum or drew his sword;
Surpass it if you can!*

*One time great General Sherman he met
And saluting he greeted his star.
The General sent the drummer boy
For a match to light his cigar.*

*General "Pap" Thomas looked thru his glass
At rugged Old Kennesaw,*

*And the boy was delighted to have him tell
All that the General saw.*

*He much admired brave General Logan
As he knew him along the way,
And he should have succeeded McPherson
Had Little Gib had his way.*

*He remembers Benjamin Harrison
Then Colonel of Volunteers,
Brigaded with the Seventy-Ninth Volunteers,
A drummer boy in the field and the band
Tho a lad in size and years.*

*Between assaults at Peach Tree Creek
Down near its flowing brim
General Newton with great glee was seen
On a log caressing him.*

*Then Little Gib with Sherman went south
By a hole that Lincoln knew;
But no one but Sherman the secret bore
The hole we would come thru.*

*Four corps in column marched away,
Little Gib the drummer along;
With thousands of Negroes on either side
To amuse with antic and song.*

*Little Gib remembers the shouting—the joy
On the march they made to the sea:
How "John Brown's Body" the soldiers sang,
And sang it spiritedly.*

*He was with Sherman's army when
They corduroyed the swamp,*

*And he went to Bentonville
Keeping Johnston on the jump.*

*When the President reviewed Sherman's army
And the crowd the soldiers espy,
What shouts and cheers they gave the two
When Gib and Fannie came by!*

*He called on President Johnston at length
Fearing he might demand
That Gib give up his Fannie Lee,
For Fannie was contraband.*

*But the President gave him the pony to keep,
Paid her passage to Wilmington, too,
And Gib and Fannie were done with war,
And home they came clear thru.*

*The youngest soldier in the army
That fought on the Union side
Came home to Clinton County
In peace with friends to abide.*

*A medal of honor his officers asked
For gallant "Little Gib,"
For many brave heroic deeds
That risked both life and rib.*

*And many a time when the Seventy-Ninth met
His name received an ovation;
But too modest he was to make a speech;
His drumming had been his oration.*

Gilbert VanZandt — 121

Historical marker in Port William, Ohio, dedicated Nov. 7, 1999, recognizing Gilbert VanZandt as an American hero. (Photo by the author)

Civil War Glossary

Bivouac A temporary military camp.
Bummer One of Sherman's troops; also used to refer to a soldier who went on an unauthorized foraging expedition.
Cavalry Soldiers trained to fight on horseback.
Civilian A noncombatant; one who isn't in the military.
Company A group or unit of soldiers.
Confiscate To seize for the government.
Contraband Forbidden goods or merchandise; during the Civil War this term also referred to former slaves that were brought across Union lines.
Corduroy road A road made of logs laid side by side.
Detail A group of soldiers ordered to carry out a particular task; a particular task.
Dispatch A message sent with speed.
Enlist To enroll in the army
Forage Search and take food or supplies
Furlough A leave of absence from duty
Grape shot Small iron balls used as cannon ammunition
Gray back A body louse.
Guerillas A small band of warriors taking part in a war independent of the main body of soldiers.
Hardtack A dry cracker, three inches square, made from flour and water.
Haversack A bag, similar to a backpack, but carried over one shoulder.
Infantry Soldiers trained to fight on foot.
Kepi A small, round, billed hat that slopes forward from the rear. Standard head gear for both sides in the Civil War.

Mess A quantity of food; a meal.
Minie ball Conical shaped bullet used during the Civil War.
Muster in/out To formally join the military service; to be formally discharged from such service.
Orderly A soldier who performs services for a superior officer.
Picket A soldier or soldiers appointed to guard the army from surprise attacks.
Quakers Religious Society of Friends; a Christian religion that emphasizes the equality of classes and sexes and a violence-free life.
Quaker gun A fake gun used to fool the enemy about the artillery strength of the army.
Quinine A bitter tonic, used as a medicine for a variety of ailments during the Civil War.
Ration A food allowance. A typical ration for a Union soldier was 1# meat, flour, hardtack, beans, rice, coffee or tea, sugar, salt, pepper, yeast, soap, candles and vinegar.
Recruit To seek to enlist; one who is enlisted.
Regiment Ten companies of 100 soldiers each, or 1000 soldiers
Reveille The drum beat or bugle call given to awaken the soldiers at daybreak.
Secesh A Confederate; short for secessionist.
Sharp shooter One who shoots with great accuracy
Sniper One who shoots at individuals from a hiding place
Skirmish A minor fight, as opposed to a full battle.
Sutler A civilian merchant who sells goods to soldiers in camp.
Tattoo A type of rhythmic drum beat.

Sources

Burnett, William G. *The Prison Camp at Andersonville.* Civil War Series. Eastern National Park and Monument A., 1995.

Castel, Albert. *The Campaign for Atlanta. Civil War Series.* Eastern National, 1996.

Davis, Burke. *Sherman's March.* New York: First Vintage Books, 1980.

-------- *The Civil War: Strange & Fascinating Facts.* New York: Wings Books, 1960.

Davis, William. *The Fighting Men of the Civil War.* London: Salamander Books Ltd., 2004.

Garrison, Web. *Civil War Curiosities: Strange Stories, Oddities, Events, and Coincidences.* Nashville: Rutledge Hill Press, 1994.

Guernsey, Alfred H. and Henry M. Alden. *Harper's Pictorial History of the Civil War.* New York: The Fairfax Press, 1866.

History of Clinton County, Ohio. Chicago: W. H. Beers & Co., 1882.

Hoar, Jay S. *Callow, Brave & True: A Gospel of Civil War Youth.* Gettysburg: Thomas Publications, 1999.

Kersey, Gary. "Gilbert VanZandt—Port William Soldier Boy.," Historical marker dedication speech, Port William, OH, Nov. 7, 1999, unpublished.

Keesee, Dennis M. *Too Young to Die, Boy Soldiers of the Union Army 1861-1865.* Huntington, West Virginia: Blue Acorn Press, 2001

Kendall, Sandra A. *Drummer Boys of the Civil War.* Gettysburg: Thomas Publications, 1998.

Linedecker, Clifford L., editor. *Civil War A to Z: The Complete Handbook of America's Bloodiest Conflict*. New York: Ballantine Books, 2002.

McCutcheon, Marc. *The Writer's Guide to Everyday Life in the 1800s*. Cincinnati: Writer's Digest books, 1993.

Miller, Francis T., editor. *The Photographic History of the Civil War*. New York, 1911.

Murphy, Jim. *The Boys' War*. N. Y: Clarion Books, 1990.

Nevin, David. *Sherman's March to the Sea*. New York: Time Life Books, 1986.

Orr, J. F. "The Story of Little Gib, Youngest Union Civil War Soldier." *The Gazette* (Xenia, OH), Feb. 28—March 8, 1938.

Robertson, James I. Jr. *The Civil War's Common Soldier*. Civil War Series. Eastern National, 1994.

Stevens, Larry. *79th Ohio Infantry*. July 7, 2001. Retrieved Oct. 21, 2002. http://www.ohiocivilwar.com/cw79.html.

Strayer, Larry M. and Richard A. Baumgartner. *Echoes of Battle: The Atlanta Campaign.* Huntington, W.V. Blue Acorn Press, 2004.

Waldron, Bob. "Youngest Soldier of Them All." *The Columbus Dispatch,* July 9, 1961, pp. 7-8.

Young, Jesse Bowman. *What a Boy Saw in the Army*. New York: Hunt and Eaton, 1894.

For more information about Ohio and the Civil War

The Ohio Memory Project is a collection of primary sources from archives, historical societies, libraries and museums that document Ohio's past from prehistory through the present. On that site, you can browse through the collection and you can create your own scrapbook. For additional information about Ohio and the Civil War, see the author's Ohio Memory Project website at

http://worlddmc.ohiolink.edu/OMP/YourScrapbook?scrapid=23326